MW00387612

# THE MAGICK OF
# FAERIES

© John A. Gold

## About the Author

Cassandra Eason is one of the most prolific and popular authors of our time, writing on all aspects of spirituality and magic in addition to lecturing, broadcasting, and facilitating workshops throughout the world. Cassandra has written ninety-four titles during the past thirty years, many of which have been translated into numerous languages, including Japanese, Russian, Hebrew, Portuguese, German, Dutch, and Spanish.

Cassandra was a teacher and university lecturer for ten years—however, her life path was to change following a vision by her three-year-old son, who accurately described a motorcycle accident in which his father was to be involved, and which subsequently occurred within minutes of the vision.

Following a great deal of research into this phenomenon, Cassandra went on to write the bestseller *The Psychic Power of Children*, the first in a long list of titles that would establish her as a worldwide bestselling author. Among her many other titles are *Angel Magic*, *Cassandra Eason's Complete Book of Spells*, *Cassandra Eason's Modern Book of Dream Interpretation*, *Contact Your Spirit Guides to Enrich Your Life*, *Crystal Healing*, *Every Woman a Witch*, and *Practical Guide to Witchcraft and Magic Spells*.

# THE MAGICK OF
# FAERIES

## Working with the Spirits of Nature

# CASSANDRA EASON

Llewellyn Publications
Woodbury, Minnesota

*The Magick of Faeries: Working with the Spirits of Nature* © 2013 by Cassandra Eason. All rights reserved. No part of this book may be used or reproduced in any manner whatsoever, including Internet usage, without written permission from Llewellyn Publications, except in the case of brief quotations embodied in critical articles and reviews.

FIRST EDITION
First Printing, 2013

Book design by Bob Gaul
Cover illustration by Aaron Pocock
Cover design by Ellen Lawson
Editing by Amy E. Quale

Llewellyn Publications is a registered trademark of Llewellyn Worldwide Ltd.

**Library of Congress Cataloging-in-Publication Data**
Eason, Cassandra.
  The magick of faeries: working with the spirits of nature/Cassandra Eason.—First Edition.
pages cm
  Includes index.
  ISBN 978-0-7387-3348-7
1. Fairies. 2. Spirits. I. Title.
  BF1552.E276 2013
  133.1'4—dc23
                          2012046583

Llewellyn Worldwide Ltd. does not participate in, endorse, or have any authority or responsibility concerning private business transactions between our authors and the public.
  All mail addressed to the author is forwarded, but the publisher cannot, unless specifically instructed by the author, give out an address or phone number.
  Any Internet references contained in this work are current at publication time, but the publisher cannot guarantee that a specific location will continue to be maintained. Please refer to the publisher's website for links to authors' websites and other sources.

Llewellyn Publications
A Division of Llewellyn Worldwide Ltd.
2143 Wooddale Drive
Woodbury, MN 55125-2989
www.llewellyn.com

Printed in the United States of America

With thanks to my literary editor and mentor, John Gold, and his wife, Kornelia, my beloved friend who inspired and encouraged me throughout this project. This book is also dedicated to my granddaughters Freya and Holly, and to Ebony and Star, the magical younger generation who confirm daily that magick is real and make me smile even through the darkest of days.

# CONTENTS

*Introduction: The Hidden Magick of Faeries and Nature Spirits*—1

**One:** Getting to Know Faeries and Nature Spirits—13

**Two:** Identifying Your Local Nature Spirits—37

**Three:** Working Magically with the Protectors
of Your Home and Workplace—57

**Four:** Magick with Traditional Faeries,
Faery Courts, and Faery Godmothers—81

**Five:** Nature Spirits of the Air—105

**Six:** Nature Spirits of the Earth—131

**Seven:** Nature Spirits of the Fire—155

**Eight:** Nature Spirits of the Water—179

**Nine:** The Fierce Creatures—205

*Appendix: The Treasury of Faery Wisdom*—227

*Suggested Reading*—241

*Index*—245

# introduction

# THE HIDDEN MAGICK OF FAERIES AND NATURE SPIRITS

## Faery Magick

Faeries and nature spirits can be fun, feisty, helpful, tiny silver-winged, gossamer light, and ethereal creatures of faery tales who grant wishes and ensure a happy ending to our current dramas. You may also encounter mischievous tricksters who offer food or gold that turns into dust in your hand as they dart away laughing, or black, hairy scary orcs with glowing coal eyes who chase you through the bushes and laugh as you scratch yourself to pieces.

## Do Faeries Exist?

Of course they do, and what can be more exciting than having an entire world, parallel to our own, sharing the same space, whose inhabitants fly and float and flit and dance in and out of view, delighting little children and perplexing our pets?

It would seem an arrogant, blinkered idea that we alone exist in the known universe. Not that nature beings care whether we believe in them. In their view, it is us—the great clodhopping humans—who share *their* space, pick their flowers and put them in vases to wither, and leave messy houses and outbuildings for the sturdy no-nonsense, overworked, and sometimes bad-tempered brownies to clear up. Indeed, try to cut the grass in a faery garden; little darts and arrows will poke at your ankles and arms (faeries love stealing silver pins to act as swords), and you will remember too late that you forgot to explain and ask permission to prune the roses.

Because faeries and nature spirits are lighter in substance than humans, they can only be seen by children or those with clairvoyant sight—unless they *choose* to appear. In this case, they appear to be as solid as you or me. A giant, however, will appear to be the size of a double-decker bus and about as dainty. Some tree spirits are excellent at camouflaging themselves so they can hardly be seen in a forest, and you may only hear chattering in the leaves or a voice on the wind—on a good day, helping you to find your way when your mobile phone tracker is out of range. On a fey's bad-hair day, they may lure you farther and farther off track into marshy land, where you panic and drop all your treasures to be added to a faery hoard. With hope, your clairvoyant sight will be so developed by the end of this book that you will be falling over faeries even in the supermarket plant section.

If you go faerie-hunting for that purpose, you can guarantee the forest will fall silent and you will be pelted with acorns and nuts from every tree. Those who need proof of faeries rely mainly on anecdotal evidence for fey folk, often carefully gathered and analysed by scholars. One of these scholars is W. Y. Evans-Wentz of Oxford University, whose research *The Faery Faith in Celtic Countries*, first published in 1890, is still a bestseller.[1] There are occasionally intriguing historical accounts witnessed by a number of people at the same time that do suggest fey folk are objectively real. One of the most intriguing accounts of actual fey people came from the twelfth century, in a place called Woolpit in Suffolk, England. It is recorded that two green-coloured children who could not speak the language suddenly appeared out of nowhere. They would eat nothing but beans and were very distressed. The boy died. It is not known what happened to the girl. Gillian Tindall, the UK author who described the incident, believes that it is possible that old races of small people might have lived in the United Kingdom until the end of the Middle Ages when the vast forests were cut down and the marshlands drained.[2]

## My Experiences with Faeries

I have always been passionate about faeries and nature spirits and remain so at the age of sixty-four. I still drive family, colleagues, and friends wild on what is supposed to be an "away from it all" trip, or en route to serious business, when I trek through acres of mud and scrub to find a faery pool or glade.

This is my third published book on nature spirits and faeries. With each one, I amass a whole lot of new accounts and experiences and frequently revise opinions I thought were so certain until I was "pixy led" to uncharted territory and realised I had accepted faery gold as facts.

I was not exactly overwhelmed by pretty little faery princesses in childhood. I grew up in the centre of an industrial town in the Midlands of England where grass was the eighth wonder of the world, with a sooty backyard and a solitary raggedy-leafed tree clinging to a mound of earth, from which my swing precariously dangled. Every Christmas my mother took me to a big department store to see Santa Claus in his grotto, where bored shop staff would dress up in tinsel and faery wings. I was totally disillusioned when I saw a faery having a cigarette behind the toadstool.

What I did not realise, as I creaked to and fro on my swing, was that the brown creatures scurrying around the tree and up and down the roses that grew around the outside toilet door, were *real* faeries. In researching the fey folk, I have discovered just how many faeries and nature spirits do live right in the middle of towns, even in potted trees in concrete shopping malls.

Hour after hour I watched the little creatures flutter their dark-brown, leaf-like wings and hop around the tree trunk playing a form of tag. My backyard fey occupied their independent world and I was even then aware I was of little more interest to them than the old ginger cat, observing them idly as he cleaned his paws.

It was not till more than forty years later I saw similar creatures around an old tree in the forests above the Gold Coast near Brisbane in Australia. It was then that I realised my childhood fey creatures were more than imagination.

During a radio broadcast in Australia, I mentioned my bush faeries to Lia, the presenter, and she told me:

*Oh, I know what they are. My brother Gary went missing in the bush for eleven days in 1984 in a place called Pannawonica when he was twenty-four years of age. Gary was freezing and had stripped some bark off the paper-bark tree and covered himself with it, like the Aboriginals did, though the wind would blow these bits away. He used this bark as a covering to stay warm during the night, though the wind would blow these bits away. One night at his lowest and coldest, the "little bushmen," as he called them, ran about him chasing the bark and tucking them all about him. He says he lay on his side and saw these "little brown beings" running about him quite quickly tucking the bark about him.*

For more than thirty years, I have researched faeries around the world and collected local fey legends passed on by word of mouth, many of them first-person anecdotes sometimes witnessed by two or more family members, but never told because of fear of ridicule. These experiences include meeting grumpy gnomes and gruesome but sometimes benign trolls in Sweden where I lived for eleven years. While there, I personally witnessed trees moving where there was no wind, the hidden *Huldra* folk, leaning over to touch me in deep pine forests. I also visited the enchanted fountains of Celtic mist-shrouded Brittany where at night beautiful white ladies frolic, the *Korrigans*, who turn into hideous hags by day. I have peered into the Ban Ban springs, home of the Australian creator rainbow serpent in North Burnett, and pursued the trail from waterhole to waterhole of the hideous water dragon-like *bunyip* who dragged young girls into the pools to be his slaves. Most fascinating are nature beings who travel with their own human clans; for example, the *Simbi*, Central African water spirits, who came to the South Carolina low countries and guarded the African slaves who were unwillingly transported from ports in West Central Africa.

# About the Book

This is far more than a book of research. The information I offer is to provide an understanding of different fey energies so you can create your own rituals and empowerments with faeries and nature spirits who will improve your life in countless ways, bringing what you most desire and need in your life. Above all, faeries can help you and your loved ones live in harmony with nature, as well as with the beings who are not only part of nature but *are* nature in animate, personalised form.

## The Difference between Faeries and Nature Beings

Just as you get beautiful porcelain-like humans and others with huge red hands, loud voices, and the ability to shoulder a load of bricks as if they were feathers, so fey magical beings vary according to the element in which they live (by that I mean earth, air, fire, or water), their size, and the role they play in the fey universe. But they are all fey or magical beings just as we are all humans in spite of our variations.

The words "fey" and "faery" (or "faerie") originally come from the Old French word *faery* that in modern French is *féerie*. The word was first used around the thirteenth or fourteenth centuries. Going back even further its roots are in the Latin *fatae*, three sisters who controlled human and divine destiny in the mythology of many lands and became the faery godmothers of every good Disney film.

Faeries tend to refer to traditional winged creatures that can vary in size from a child's little finger to stately shimmering figures that are talented in arts and music and live in crystalline, subterranean royal courts. Some, such as the light elves of Scandinavia, are associated with high places. You have encountered light elves if you have read J. R. R. Tolkien's *Lords of the Rings*. They are slightly smaller than humans and rather more beautiful than your average size-zero human fashion model; they have pointed faces and shimmering eyes.

In contrast, nature spirits are the workers of the fey world, resembling and caring for the element or natural feature where they live, such as trees or waterfalls. They often take names and their characteristics from their habitat. Faeries, even in their most ethereal stately form, are different from angels, though both are spiritual beings. While there are a number of accounts described in this book, including the one of Greg in the previous section, of how faeries will help humans in trouble, they are not one hundred percent beings of light and goodness dedicated to serve humans as are angels. Fey beings have their own agenda and are not there to serve humans. They can be very unpredictable and at times spiteful, a reason why I describe ways of protecting yourself while working with the best and most benign of the faeries and fey energies.

## Faery Magick

As previously stated, faeries are not just part of nature, but *are* nature. There are four main kinds of fey energies relating to the four main kinds of fey beings, and each has its own kind of magick.

The first kind is earth, which includes the beings of the forests, meadows, rocks, crystals, and plant energies. There are often earth faeries in mines; for example, the Bolivian *El Tio* mine spirit who receives offerings of cocoa, cigarettes, alcohol and llama blood to ensure protection and good fortune for the miners.

The second kind is air for all ambitions, wishes, and dreams. They are usually winged spirits of sky, mountains, winds, and weather, such as the tall winged sylphs who are so protective of their mountains.

The third kind is fire for passion, inspiration, creativity, and fast-moving matters. They include the spirits of the hearth fires, bonfires, and the desert *djinns*, commonly known as "genies of the lamp."

Most varied are the creatures of the waters, from gentle mermaids to fierce *bokwus*. The bokwus is a Native American male spirit found near rushing water in North American spruce, larch, and fir forests; they bring love and reconciliation but can also wash away feelings that are destructive or no longer wanted, such as guilt and fear.

Fey magick can be cast in natural settings, backyards, on balconies of city apartments, or indoors by a potted plant, which can be as rich in spirits as any untamed forest.

But enough of talk. Let's try two basic fun but very effective fey rituals.

## Activity: Bringing Wishes into Actuality through Spellcasting with Faery Energy

When we are children, we know anything is possible and ask the faeries to grant our wishes, which often they do, even if in unexpected ways. In actuality, children tap into innate psychic powers people have known about and used since cave times. We all possess psychokinesis, or mind power with the ability to draw to us what we need and repel what is potentially harmful. This power is demonstrated again and again in every wand-waving faery godmother tale and anecdotal account of faeries granting wishes for mortals. The fey ability to grant wishes is no different from modern scientific theories of energy we read about in bestselling books such as *The Secret* by Rhonda Byrne. For if we reach out for what we most want as though it is already ours and remove self-imposed limitations, we can move the parcel of energy containing what we most need from the thought plane into our lives through the power of words and actions to stir those energies.

Fey magick shortcuts doubts. Through simple wish rituals, it generates the impetus to launch our needs and desires into the cosmos so they bounce back into our lives fulfillable and fulfilled. This inrush of fey power not only draws your desires and needs to you, but guides you automatically toward your particular opportunity.

## Wish Magick in Practice

Wish magick is associated particularly with air faeries as wishes are released into the cosmos, though you can also burn wishes and activate the fire essences you may often see as shadows or in sparks around a bonfire. There are also earth wishes that are slow growing if planted as images scratched on stones beneath thriving garden or pot plants, and water wishes as you release petals as offerings off a bridge, launching your desires into a fast-flowing stream.

## A Basic Air Fey Wish Ritual

Air faeries may travel as butterflies, dandelion seeds, or thistledown. Although gardeners and farmers do not welcome the practice, children as well as young lovers have blown dandelion clocks and sent faeries on their way, making wishes at the same time.

This is a good loosening-up exercise if the logical adult mindset intrudes.

- When you see thistledown or a dandelion clock, blow it softly, three breaths for each blow, and help the air folk on their way. As you do so, concentrate on a venture of your own or a dream that you would like to set in motion.

- Half-close your eyes until you can see or visualise each of the feathery spores as tiny wings flying into the air and recite the wish three times.

- Repeat your wish three times as you blow each subsequent set of spores, each time softly blowing three times to release each set of spores.

- If there are no spores nearby, visit a butterfly farm and choose a butterfly each time you make a wish. Again blow softly three times for each butterfly and whisper or say the wish softly three times for every chosen butterfly.

- The key is to release the wish, let go of expectations and doubts, and trust the fey to carry the wishes to the cosmos for transformation.

- With both spores and butterflies, focus on one wish that can be personal, for someone else, or environmental.

- Afterward, leave an offering. In the butterfly park, the offering could be a dish of nectar or a donation to conservation work. If you are using spores, your can pick up litter, leave some crystal chips in a small dish, or plant seeds on waste land. Do not leave hematite, iron, tiger iron, or any other crystal that contains iron; faeries hate iron.

Now let's try one more wish spell.

## A Faery Dust Wish

In the faery lore of old Ireland, it was believed if you found glittering faery dust, fallen from the cloak of the beautiful faery Queen Oonagh whose white gown shone with pearls and diamonds, any wish would be granted.[3]

If you are casting the wish spell indoors or on a paved area, use faery dust or glitter that can be purchased in a tiny phial at New Age stores; alternatively, use any tube of silver glitter. When outdoors, substitute rose petals, dried lavender, or dried rosemary (known as the "faery herb") to avoid damaging the environment.

### You will need:

A small tube of silver glitter or a dish of rose petals, lavender, rosemary, or any small white or pink petals.

### Timings:

Perform the spell when you wake in the morning. If you can find a faery ring or a natural circle of toadstools or mushrooms, the spell is doubly powerful, but you can cast the spell in any area where the vegetation is long or wild or within a circle of trees or bushes; alternatively cast it in a paved or indoor uncarpeted area and create a circle of green potted plants to work within. If the dew is on the grass, it is even better.

### The spell:

- If you are not within a natural circle, define one in your mind surrounding you and mark its limits in visualized light; you can do this with a clear, rose quartz, or amethyst crystal wand or use the index finger of your dominant hand. Massage wands are ideal.

- With yourself at the center of the imagined fey circle, turn clockwise (if you live in the Northern Hemisphere) with the crystal wand in your dominant hand, your arm extended and horizontal; turn counter-clockwise if you live in the Southern Hemisphere.

• Visualise light extending from the wand or finger to create a circle of shimmering light from the ground up to waist height so the light gradually becomes mistier as it rises. Say, "I welcome the fair folk of earth and sky into this enchanted grove and respectfully ask your blessings." Traditionally the word "faeries" was not used directly in addressing or speaking of the fey in Celtic countries but instead euphemisms such as "Mother's Blessings" or the "Small People."

• In a physical tree circle, walk just within the perimeter in both directions as above saying, "I welcome the fair folk of earth and sky into this enchanted grove and respectfully ask your blessings."

• Holding your tube of glitter or bowl of petals in your dominant hand, walk around the perimeter of the circle nine more times in alternate clockwise and counter-clockwise directions, beginning clockwise in the Northern Hemisphere and counter-clockwise in the Southern Hemisphere. Recite your wish in your head or aloud, continually as a soft mantra, slowly and evenly. Try to reduce it to five or six words.

• Go to the centre of the circle and call your wish once aloud as you scatter a little of the faery dust or petals and ask the fair folk to grant your request if and when it is right to be.

• Turn in the reverse direction you began casting the circle of light with your wand or walk the actual circle once more and say, "I thank the fair folk of earth and sky and ask them to carry my wishes within the enchanted circle to fulfilment within the world in which I live and share so willingly with you."

• Walk out of the circle. Do not look back.

• Save the rest of the glitter for other wishes, but cast any herbs or petals to the winds.

In the next chapter, we will create a faery place and learn more about the fey or magical people who allow us to share their space.

---

## Introduction Sources

1. Evans-Wentz, W. Y. *The Faery Faith in Celtic Countries.* Lemma, NY: Lemma Books, 1973. Evinity Publishing, 2009. Kindle version.

2. Tyndall, Gillian. *A Handbook of Witches.* Plymouth: Mayflower Press, 1972.

3. Wilde, Lady. *Legends, Charms, and Superstitions of Ireland.* Mineola: Dover Publications, 2006.

# I

GETTING TO KNOW FAERIES
AND NATURE SPIRITS

The most effective way to discover the world of the fey is to spend time in nature, listening and observing the moving grasses, trees, waters. Sure signs of fey activity might be a sudden flattening of the grass when there is no wind or chattering and whispering that goes silent if you follow its direction. A dog or very small child who suddenly becomes still and stares intently is another indicator of the presence of the "Little People." Nature spirits will come to you if you are patient; if you visit the same spot regularly you may come to recognise the fey who live there (more of this in chapter 2).

## Accessing the World of the Fey

Faeryland is instantly accessible on those occasions when a doorway appears in the dimensions between the two worlds, for example the space between two trees in misty sunlight, in ancient sacred places on any of the seasonal change points, or during magical festivals. The most magical is the space between two oak trees or where oak, ash, and thorn grow together. May Eve (November 1, called "Beltane" in the Southern Hemisphere) and Hallow-een traditionally are the times when the faeries move from their winter to summer quarters and back again and so are very visible to humans at dawn and twilight. Mischievous faeries can be a problem on Halloween; on May Eve in the Northern Hemisphere, standing stones and ancient rocks are said to open and fey revelry and music can be heard from within.

Midsummer is also an occasion when faeryland and the mortal world move closer. At Midsummer, or the "Summer Solstice" in the old calendar (around December 20 in the Northern Hemisphere and June 20 in the Southern), a golden doorway appears at noon in the centre of stone circles and old medicine wheels and the otherworld may be clearly viewed.

At any time and season, when we are quiet and in harmony with the natural world, which could be a park or wildlife garden in a city, we may become suddenly aware of the presence of fey beings coexisting as the two worlds momentarily merge. Our personal aura energy field radiating from our body in seven rainbow bands, an ellipse all around us, is made of the same essential substance as the bodies of faeries and nature spirits. Young children see faeries everywhere; the winged-type of fey beings are especially attracted to them.

## Faery Encounters

Many adults  recall  faery experiences in childhood. During my research on children's psychic experiences at the Alister Hardy Research Centre in Oxford, England, I found that people in their seventies and eighties would say that those childhood experiences, too often dismissed as fantasy, remain as real so many years later. One individual, Julie, is now in her forties and described an experience of seeing faeries as a child at the Ventnor Botanic Garden on the Isle of Wight, which is very close to a major ley or earth energy line beneath the land. Ley lines, sometimes called faery paths in Ireland, are a natural source of power that seem to make it easier for people to see faeries. Julie told me:

*I have a very vivid memory of an experience I had as a child when on holiday. It was around 1968 when I was about five years old. I was walking ahead of my parents when I was amazed to see very small human-formed beings—not more than a foot high—running very quickly beside us along the path. I do not recall if they had wings, but they moved so fast.*

Only Julie saw the faeries, though parents do occasionally see faeries simultaneously with their child, especially if the parent is very open spiritually.

Yet, even in adulthood, faeries can appear quite spontaneously to sensitive adults. Mark wrote to me:

*I was staying with my parents at the village of Wickhambishops in Essex [UK] where I grew up. One of my favourite places to visit was a nature reserve in between the villages of Little Baxstead and Great Baxstead. At the time, I was around twenty-three years old. I had a lot on my mind and often visited this particular site as it always helped me to recharge my batteries and put everything into perspective. I was walking through a series of foot paths in the reserve, and I would stop and pick up litter while following the trail. Suddenly, I had an overwhelming compulsion that I was not alone. I looked up and saw what looked like a small faery, comparable to the size of a squirrel, hovering above me in front of a tree about two metres away and six metres above me. As soon as I looked up the faery saw me, looked at me for a few seconds, then darted to a new location across the trail a few metres away, where it looked at me again and then darted out of sight. The faery looked like a long-haired female and had four wings. I thought it had natural skin-coloured clothes on but as it moved so fast I can't be sure.*

*To satisfy my curiosity after walking a bit further along the footpath, trying to dismiss the experience as imagination, I turned around and walked back along the footpath looking for the faery. I saw it again and it did exactly the same thing. The second time it was lower down and hovering in some bushes. Once again it froze briefly when it saw me, and then flew off. Incidentally the nature reserve contains some kind of tumuli or burial mound located in the woods. The last time I saw the faery, it darted toward the supposed location of the mound. At university, I trained as a scientist so I have always been trained to look at things objectively.*

We can make fey encounters more likely if, like Mark, we act in a way that is pleasing to the fey. Mark always picked up litter, as that is an increasing problem for countryside that has become partly urbanised. That is a modern version of faery offerings and wins favour with the fey, as does participation in tree-planting schemes and polluted river or canal reclamation. Also, there was an ancient burial mound very close to where Mark saw the faery and these ancient sites were invariably built on centres of powerful earth energies, often where ley lines cross. Such places invariably attract more faeries than ordinary sites.

## Bringing the Fey into Your Everyday World

Of course we cannot always commune with nature daily. However, by setting up a fey centre in your home, garden, balcony, or backyard, you can ensure that nature spirits of all kinds, not just household guardians of whom I write in chapter 3, will bless your home and immediate environs with their presence. Once you welcome fey energies into your daily life, a practice that has been largely forgotten in modern society, you will become luckier and more prosperous. As you open your home to the spontaneous energies of faeries and nature spirits, abundance in health and joy will flow in.

This fey centre will give you a source of fresh energies like a gentle breeze blowing through your home and your life. Visitors will ask whether you have redecorated and family members will become more enthusiastic and less confrontational. If you do not have a garden area, you can collect a small group of portable items so that you can create outdoor faery places wherever you go. Because I am a frequent traveler, I often make mini fey sets to put in luggage for hotel rooms.

## Creating a Fey Centre in Your Home

I described in the introduction how faeries can be divided into four main categories according to whether they are earth, air, fire, or water beings. Even simple magick works with these four main elements, or more accurately, energies. When they are combined, they create a fifth powerful energy sometimes called *Aether* or *Akasha* in which the centre of the circle will form a vortex allowing wishes to be transformed into actuality.

Most spells and rituals use the circle formation. In fey magick, the four elements often manifest as four nature spirits, one for each element, who are invited into the circle.

## Identifying the Elements in Your Fey Place

- Rather than following traditional directional positions of conventional magick that will vary according to location, *feel* where the four different elements are within the circle, whether you visualise the circle outdoors, mark it with a stick in soil, or mark it with stone markers at regular intervals (eight is common).

- Outdoors, use your bare feet and hands with palms flat and facing downwards to make connection with the four very different sensations.

- Indoors, use a circular table and either hold your hands (palms down) over the fey table or use a pendulum to identify the four energy positions by its positive swing (you would say to the pendulum, "show me the air quadrant").

- The quadrants will be divided approximately evenly. Earth will *feel* solid and heavy. Air will feel rippling and light, and you might feel the sensation of a slight breeze. Fire will be warm, dynamic, and will make you feel excited. Water will feel flowing and very cool. The centre is the mixture of all four and feels very still and harmonious. You will get an overlap of energies where one quadrant gives way to the other.

## Indoors:

- Use a small table covered with a cloth you can change according to the seasons—brown for winter, yellow for spring, orange or red for summer, and blue for autumn. If you live in a region where there are wet and dry seasons, use blue or green for the wet season and yellow or orange for the dry.

- Hang a faery or nature spirit picture or a scene of natural beauty on a wall above your fey place.

- In the center, set a beautiful, serene, tall, and slender fey or nature spirit statue or the image of a nature god or goddess, such as the ancient Greek woodland Pan or the huntress Artemis. This should be all natural material (nothing artificial) made from wood, bronze, copper, silver (loved by fey people), or ceramic; certainly, do not anything containing iron.

Use appropriate symbols for each of the four elements. The symbol is usually placed halfway around the individual quadrant touching the perimeter.

- Earth can be represented by a rock, unpolished crystal, or mineral; for example, an amethyst geode with tiny crystals embedded within, a green plant, or small ceramic bowl of dried herbs such as thyme. (Thyme is said to make it easier to see faeries, and should be sprinkled around windows and doorways to attract benign faeries to your home.)

- Air can be signified by a feather or smudge stick.

- Fire can be represented by a glass bowl containing glass nuggets or shining clear quartz crystals; alternatively, a small candle made of natural beeswax or vegetable base (not paraffin).

- Water can represented by a seashell or a small dish of aquamarine or coral, the sea-spirit stones.

- Place a small bowl made of wood or ceramic in the centre of the table, in which you will place offerings.

- Put a second small bowl in the centre to collect any special berries, unusual flowers or leaves, feathers, nuts, seeds, sea shells, or twigs that you find to have a magical appearance, and tiny natural bark sculptures that have fallen to the ground. These you should replace regularly to keep fresh. Sometimes you will sense something is not for you, even if you find it fallen; trust this instinct, for it may be the spirit is not ready to release it.

- Because the fey love sparkle, put faery crystals, pearls, precious and Andean opals, Australian boulder opals, chiastolite, staurolite, or faery crosses in a dish. Silver, copper, bronze (an alloy of copper and tin), tin, and gold are also acceptable metals to faeries. Real silver pins are especially loved so the faeries might have something sharp to cut with. Iron and steel, however, are so hated and feared by them. In his book, *Golden Bough: A Study in Magick and Religion*, folklorist and scholar Sir James Frazer describes how iron should be wedged in the door of a faery dwellings to prevent them from shutting in humans.[1]

- You can add whatever you wish to your faery place, but do not overcrowd it. Keep it well dusted and fresh, as faeries hate clutter. Use only natural materials.

## Outdoors:

- Ideally, find a small sheltered part of the garden where indigenous wildflowers and herbs grow with a natural circle of bushes or plants to mark your faery circle. Here you can have a faery house and faery door (some people have a faery door, a miniature wooden door, propped in their indoor fey place as well). If you do have one outdoors, wedge it in a hollow of a tree or between two bushes embedded in the ground, rather than using nails or screws. The doors are usually small and though you can buy beautifully ornate painted ones from faery stores or crafts people at festivals, plain doors in a faery wood, such as hawthorn, oak, or apple harmonise better with the natural energies. Elder wood, sacred to the fae, is never cut, burned, or harmed even if fallen.

• Leave a tiny woven basket near the faery door or a natural hollow in a tree; in the basket, put tiny pearls (from old necklaces), small shells, or crystal chippings. Faeries (except for dwarves, gnomes, mine or subterranean spirits, and sea mothers) generally do not like coins except for old ones made of tin, bronze, or silver (the kind you can get in museum stores). If you want to leave food, since fey only take the essence, offer seeds or small fruits that can be shared by birds or wildlife. You can add offerings whenever you seek the blessings of the fey. When your basket overflows, allow the older offerings to spill on to the ground to be absorbed or adorn the earth.

• Faery houses are optional. Some people make a small, simple shelter from twigs and leaves. They are like miniature bivouacs in the centre of the fey place where there is a tree or tree stump, or they are placed near one of the edges. Some household spirits may adopt a child's doll house or bird house, especially if made from natural wood. You can easily make one, the less elaborate the better. There are several excellent online sites and books to give you ideas if you want to make your own.[2]

• As with all magick, you are more likely to attract the fey if you use local materials. In Maine, there is a one hundred-plus year old tradition of gnome houses to protect livestock and children during the winter. These little houses contain a coin for the Little People. You could use the stump of a tree as a base or build against a hollow using clay, sticks, feathers, and pine cones. If near the shore, driftwood and shells are ready materials. Be as ingenious as you like, as a rudimentary leaf bed may be more acceptable to earth spirits than a miniature doll bed. Children are excellent at creating, and a simple faery house is easier to rebuild after bad weather.

• If you do not have a garden, you can create a fey site in a local woodland or quiet park area using the surrounding natural tools. Usually, the house and your site markings will be there on subsequent visits if you choose a sheltered place off the main track.

• For the four quadrants, you may find an area with four natural markers such as bushes in woodland. In a permanent garden site, use four small stone or weatherproofed wooden or bronze statues of the fey.

• You may find a small gnome for earth, a winged figure for air, a reddish stone figure for fire, and perhaps a faery next to a small pool for the water element. If the site is not permanent, keep miniature statues in a fey bag that can be easily carried. Alternatively, use four stone or wooden animals, a badger or rabbit for earth, an eagle or butterfly for air, a fox or stag for fire and a dolphin or fish for water.

• Decorate the circle with feathers, flowers, and leaves if you wish and put water and a small offerings dish in the centre. Also in the centre, if the fey house is not there, place a larger fey figure, dragon, or unicorn for the mystical element. You can adorn a temporary circle outdoors and allow the winds to blow away what they wish between visits. You may find others add to your circle in your absence, especially if it is a public place; this will enhance rather than detract from the energies.

# Blessing and Empowering Your Fey Places

- Before beginning and after ending any fey ritual, anoint the centre of your brow with three drops of water either collected from rain that has not touched the ground or a bubbling tap that has run for a minute. Say, "By earth, sea, and sky may I be protected from all that is not from the light and of good intention."

- The first time you use the indoor fey altar and each Friday (the day of the faeries) thereafter, light a candle and add a small cedar, sagebrush, or rosemary/thyme smudge stick on the altar. Light the smudge stick, and blow gently until the tip of the smudge is glowing and there is a steady stream of smoke. Open any windows if the space is confined. If you prefer, you can use a natural thyme, pine, rosemary, or lavender incense stick.

- Slowly weave above the whole table with spirals of smoke as though weaving a web, while rhythmically saying softly and continuously, "You wise ones of earth, sky, fire, and water, weave now your magick blessings in this place. Bring health, peace, and abundance into my home and make this your home, a dwelling place of joy and harmony. Blessings be always with you."

- Leave the smudge and the candle to burn through and each day add a small offering, having tidied the table and replaced any stale offerings.

- Repeat the blessing daily using your hands (palms horizontal, flat, and facing downward over the table). In a steady rhythm, move your right hand clockwise and the left hand counterclockwise. In both cases, you will know when the magical web has been woven, generally after about nine chants. Each day, you can ask for a blessing and name some kindness you will perform in return.

- For your outdoor place, make sure everything is neat and clean and replace any food offerings that are decaying. You can bury the old ones.

- The first time you empower your outdoor place, whether permanent or temporary, and thereafter whenever you go there, find the closest natural twig or a pointed stone that will serve as a wand. With the wand in your hand, walk around the outside of the circle, first clockwise for the Northern Hemisphere or counterclockwise for the Southern Hemisphere, reversing the direction after each circuit and using any bushes or trees as natural markers. Keep the wand or stone pointed downwards at a forty-five-degree angle and say continuously as you make nine circuits, "You wise ones of this grove, I ask your presence, I seek your blessings. I come in respect leaving only my footprints and my offerings. I offer in return to do the most good with the highest of intentions."

- When you have finished, sit in the centre of your circle with your eyes closed and receive wisdom from the spirits of the trees, the breeze, or the whispering plants. You may hear this externally or within your mind.

- Then leave the circle picturing a doorway of light and say, "The circle of the wise ones shall remain unbroken. I leave only my footprints, my offerings, and my thanks for your presence."

- Return the stick or stone to where you found it, make a small offering and say, "I give thanks for this borrowing. All is as it was before. Blessings be on all until we meet again."

## Visiting the Land of the Fey

In addition to inviting the fey into our world, we can visit the land of fey in a light meditative state. People have done this for hundreds of years as they sat on faery hills or mounds. Indeed, you can be sure if you come across a landmark with the word "faery" in its name you have come across one such place, even if it is now in the middle of a housing development.

The faery world is akin to the dream world, for though we see faeries and nature spirits in woodlands or other natural earthly settings, they in fact occupy the vibrational spirit space between the material human world and the angels, sometimes called the second celestial plane of existence. This spiritual realm is called the astral plane and is one level more ethereal than the innermost etheric plane we visit in our dreams, the spiritual dimension that is closest to the everyday world. Its coloured ray or the magical light in which it is bathed is pink-rose coloured.

Perceiving this realm is like suddenly seeing through the hole in a misty curtain. To access this fey space or vibration in which faery magick takes place, and not only see but pass through the dimensional curtain, sit in a sheltered place in a garden or indoors near an open window. Alternatively, work in your indoor or outdoor fey place; the more you use them, they will gain power and reveal their own gateways to faeryland.

## Visiting the Fey in Meditation

- Burn a rose-coloured candle and myrrh, carnation or rose incense, or use a rose-scented candle. These are associated with the astral or fey plane.

- Look into the flame to connect with the world of faery, nature spirits, and also magical talking animals as the flame expands and becomes a golden doorway.

- Close your eyes and picture the candle flame within your mind's vision, filling a misty-pink rose colour screen and the flame opening to create a magical golden doorway in the shimmering rose light. Imagine the land around you falling away to take you directly into the land of fey.

- Once you have found the doorway, walk through it into a beautiful emerald-green forest. The pathways are overhung with trees loaded with golden fruits and there are multicoloured butterflies, rainbow birds, and fragrant, richly coloured exotic flowers.

- You will find a particular faery or nature spirit waiting inside the doorway to act as your guide, and in time this nature spirit guide will be able to answer your questions or show you what you most need to see. Follow the nature spirit; because you are in a meditative or dream state, nothing can harm you. In traditional fey encounters on the physical plane, do not eat or drink anything, take any faery gifts, ride on faery horses, attempt to enter a faery ring, or dance in faery revels. Decline politely, as less benign fey may take advantage and make you dance till you are exhausted or get a soaking as a faery horse unexpectedly plunges into water.

- You can talk to anyone—magical animals, tree spirits, and, with respect, faery kings and queens. With the help of your guide, you will fly, float, and go deep into tree roots to magical kingdoms and watch the fey painting flowers or playing their fabulous golden instruments.

- When it is time to go home, the scene will usually fade; if not, look for a golden doorway in a nearby tree, thank your guide, pass through it and you will become aware of the sights and sounds of the everyday world. The everyday world will gradually surround you, but do not be in too much of a hurry to return to daily life. If you wish, glimpse back through the doorway and then again at the candle flame.

- Scribble down, draw, or paint your experiences and any special magical creatures you encountered. Record these in your faery journal that I will describe in the next chapter. By the time you have finished reading my book, you should have one of your own.

## Warnings about Faery Encounters

Though in meditation nothing can harm you and fey presences you encounter are always benign, nature spirits are generally like young children emotionally and can be volatile, turning from laughter to unprovoked fury in seconds (see chapter 9). You are dealing with spirits of the wild winds and the turbulent waters, the leaping fire and the earth that can shudder and shake security. The real danger is that these spirits can bring out the worst in us, unless we are aware of this and only ever carry out fey rituals when we are calm and positive.

The ambivalence of faeries and their powerful telepathic abilities enable them to magnify your mood, so if you are feeling angry, jealous, or resentful, fey energies will make you feel that you can and should get your own back on those who have offended you, which may not be wise. We have to be even more moral with faery magick than other types of magick; unlike angel magick, with faery magick you do not have the built-in goodness of the angels to protect you from your own less-worthy thoughts or discourage you from acting unwisely.

## Using Good Faery Magick to Overcome Problems

In fey spellcasting, you can and should ask for the strength to leave a destructive situation or to bind a bully threatening harm to you or someone you love. You can ask that justice be granted to you in the way and time that is right, harming none, and that what is rightfully yours to be returned. That way, you draw the best of the nature spirits' energies into your spell and amplify the powers of light and goodness that are ultimately stronger than any darker powers, fey or mortal.

## Asking Permission

Unless you are working in your own magical place, it is important to seek permission to be present with the fey and to practice your ritual even with the best-intentioned fey magick, as nature spirits are temperamentally volatile. Be sensitive to the atmosphere and be alert to cold breezes or a sense of unwelcome. If the energies feel wrong, move on or try another day. If in doubt, spiral a pendulum over the area where you intend to work; if it spins out of control, if your fingers feel cold, or it is as if you are experiencing a mild electric shock, then this is not a place for you to practice magick at this particular time.

Phred wrote about her local faery wood and how she learned that asking permission of the nature spirits worked wonders.

*Here in urban London, my local park (really the bottom end of Epping For-est) has a bluebell wood and also a rather impenetrable "proper" faery wood.*

*I found that every time I entered the faery wood with a distracted mind, I would get tangled up in the brambles and hurt myself, or end up at a dead end and have to find my way out again. I quickly realised that I was far from alone in this part of the wood though there were no humans, and started asking permission of the nature spirits to enter—and the injuries and get-ting lost stopped.*

*One day, having brought a small gift and having meditated, I found myself just sitting and watching as the air filled with sparkle and as I looked around, I perceived a small, dancing blue light circling around me. I had actually seen my first faery with open eyes!*

## Discovering the Power of Faery Glamour

Using fey glamour is a love, fame, or success-attraction ritual. Faery glam-our is an often misunderstood but very effective faery power we can use to increase our natural charisma and the confidence to attract love, create good impressions, and be noticed in a positive way.

The original term "glamour" in modern times can describe either a person where makeup, clothes, fast cars, and expensive yachts create the appearance that the person lives a wonderful life (which may or may not be true). Glam-our comes from the Scottish word *glaumerie*, which means "magick."

Faeries, elves, and other fey folk have the ability to create illusions of won-derful feasts and faery gold which mortals might come across as they travel lonely tracts of land at night. These turn to dust or ashes when seized, con-sumed, or bathed in the morning light. Tales abound of young men who were seduced by a beautiful faery maiden, only to find when they woke in the morn-ing she was a hideous hag. The English Oxford scholar W. Y. Evans-Wentz, who traveled through Wales, Ireland, Scotland, the Isle of Man, Cornwall, and Brittany from 1908 to 1910, obtained firsthand experiences of people who described many such experiences.

Other fey forms such as the will o' the wisps, whom I describe in chapter 7 on fire spirits, could make pathways appear across marshy lands to mislead travelers; he could lead them to follow a dancing light deep into boggy land or even quicksand. So it may be that the palaces of crystal and gold of the courtly fey were in fact just illusions to lure young men and women to become the lovers of amorous faery kings and queens; when the mortal men and women would find themselves alone on a cold hillside after what seemed to be only one night of wonder in faeryland, it would be revealed that decades had passed in the mortal world. Conversely beautiful faery palaces could be perceived by curious mortals as just a pile of rocks if the fey chose to remain unseen or considered those passing by unworthy of such beauty. The Welsh *Bendith y Mamau,* whose name means "Mother's Blessing" (a euphemism sometimes applied to other lake ladies to avert their less benign tendency to kidnap children), were a mixture of the *Tylwyth Teg* (the "fair family"), golden lake ladies, and ugly goblins. They used glamour to appear beautiful and seduce mortals, as did the Scandinavian *Huldra* earth spirits who magically disguised their cow tails and hollow backs.

## A Glamour Ritual

Glamour does not have to be used for deception. By using faery crystals, we can adapt fey glamour to enhance our own charisma and self-confidence, giving us an extra boost when we doubt ourselves, when others are being nasty, or when we need to sell ourselves at a job interview. You may not be aware of your potential because others have wrongly told you that you are unattractive or stupid to boost their own egos; glamour will allow you to see yourself clearly, to enhance performance, and make you shine in the world even if you are scared inside.

### Glamour and Crystals

Each crystal contains a guardian spirit. Fey crystals especially have energies that are related to the shining faeries (see the Faery Treasury in the appendix for a full list of faery crystals). Because crystals have such powerful aura energy fields, they are ideal for taking the most positive aspects of glamor into yourself.

The more glamour rituals you do, the more the outer appearance becomes the reality and you project those strengths as well as feel radiant and brave inside. Many people fear their own power and charisma; they hide it behind awkwardness, and so glamour rituals are incredibly liberating.

This rite is most powerful on the night of the full moon or any Sunday at noon (the day of Michael, Archangel of the Sun), depending on whether you are using a sun or moon crystal. Moon crystals are better for love and enhancing beauty and sun crystals for fame and outer success or courage. You can use sun or moon crystals at different times for inner and outer power.

- Take two pearls, two creamy moonstones, or two pieces of silky white selenite, all fey moon crystals. Alternatively, use two shimmering yellow citrines or two sparkling clear quartz, both kinds of fey sun crystals.

- According to the stones you choose, stand in sunshine or clear light or moonlight. If the weather is bad, use a gold candle for the sun and a silver candle for the moon.

- Hold one crystal in each hand and softly breathe on each crystal three times, first on the left-hand crystal and then the right-hand one, to make the connection between the crystalline energies and your own energy field that runs through your chakras and out through your aura.

- Stand where your reflection shines in a mirror or pool of water and you can see the sun or moon or candlelight also reflected.

- State what powers you need to radiate through your aura energy field. Then say, "May my light shine forth gloriously into the world by the power of the fey."

- Raise your arms over your head and spiral the crystals a few centimeters above your hair, and then circle the two crystals a few centimeters away from your face, down to your forehead, across your eyes and ears and up again over your head and around your shoulders in a steady rhythm.

• Make progressively wider circles until both crystals are an extended arm span around your head and shoulders, the extent of the average human aura, all the time chanting softly and mesmerically, "May my light shine forth gloriously into the world by the power of the fey. Wind bind enchantment in, weave and leave no trace of sadness. Spin and spiral, joy from sorrow. Bright as star glow, silver moonlight, sunlit gold, faery glamour I unfold."

• Spin around nine times in alternate directions, three clockwise, three counterclockwise, and three clockwise if you live in the Northern Hemisphere and reversing the spins for the Southern Hemisphere.

• Finally, shake the crystals nine times in your closed hands, toss the crystals in the air and catch them, to release the energies into your aura.

• Afterward, to cleanse the crystals, smudge them in spirals with a small sagebrush stick or incense of sage, rose, or lavender. Keep all your glamour crystals in a drawstring bag with a sprig of mint so you can repeat the ritual whenever you need glamour, using the appropriate candle for your chosen crystals.

## Fey Methods of Stepping Beyond Linear Time and Physical Distance

Astral fey shape-shifting or mind travel is an easily learned magical technique to increase your personal power. This technique improves your ability to think outside the box, your tunnel vision, creativity, and inspiration, especially in the arts and predictive abilities.

J. M. Barrie wrote of Peter Pan in his novel *The Little White Bird* [3] in 1902 when he first introduced the character and mythology of Peter Pan: "The moment you doubt you can fly, you cease forever to be able to do it. The only reason birds can fly and we can't is because they have perfect faith, because to have perfect faith is to have wings."

Soul flight or mind flight enables us to fly like faeries and with the faeries. It is immensely liberating if your creativity is blocked or you need to free yourself from a stagnant situation or relationship.

The adult fey soul that gives us spontaneity at any age as well as the ability to travel beyond the physical body in mind or astral travel is part of our spiritual body and this is what Barrie was talking about. This rainbow spirit body, which is the blueprint of our perfect ideal self, spills out as the rainbow energy aura field around us. As I already mentioned, this aura is of the same spiritual vibration as faeries. This spirit body enters our physical body before or during birth and leaves the body at the end of life as pure light, as has been attested in many eyewitness accounts of those who have shared a loved one's last moments.

Children, until about the age of five, routinely report experiences of being able to float downstairs, fly, or make their rainbow body dance in front of them.[4] This is done using the fey part of their soul.

Adults can rediscover fey flight, thus restoring what may be long overdue joy and spontaneity. Peter Pan recommends faith, trust, and the gold pixie dust he shook from his tiny faery companion Tinkerbell so Wendy and her brothers could fly to Neverland.

## Fey Flight for Grown Ups

Fey flight is much lighter and subtler than traditional Shamanic bird flight. The easiest way to begin your fey flying is in sunlight, using your shadow as the stimulus. The shadow represents a part of ourselves that is free to dance and move ahead or behind us according to the angle of the sun. Spiritually, the shadow holds hidden or undeveloped parts of ourselves that offer great potential for happiness when released.

- Wear an outfit with long flowing sleeves so when you raise your arms your shadow has natural fey wings.

- Begin in an open space such as a meadow or open grassland where the air spirits and winged faeries fly freely and where there are birds, butterflies, and dragonflies as the season permits.

- Find a lightly coloured path on a slight incline and walk toward the morning or early evening sun, the times of day when shadows are at their clearest and longest.

- Turn suddenly so the sun is behind you and greet your shadow in front of and slightly above you (experiment).

- This shadow is the physiological manifestation of your vibrant reawakened spirit self that can step outside the physical body and merge with the sunlight.

- As you lift your arms high on either side of your head, you will see your shadow self's wings.

- Feel the air all around and by turning around and around rapidly, create a sense of lightness. Blow bubbles from a giant bubble blower and focus on one of the rising bubbles.

- Wave, dance and lift one leg, then the other.

- Jump as if you were a child again with both feet so your shadow flies. Then turn from side to side rapidly, so the shadow is first one side and then the other; swirl around and around, peeping at the shadow first billowing behind and then in front of you.

- Move so your shadow is in front of you again and jump with your arms raised. Project a positive thought to the shadow; watch as the shadow instantaneously tosses it back.

• When you are ready, walk into a shady area where your shadow disappears. Lie down and look upward, focusing on a particular area of clouds or blue sky.

• Now close your eyes and see the sky getting closer in your mind.

• Count aloud very slowly and rhythmically from twelve down to one, and then as slowly upward in the same rhythm from one to thirteen.

• At each of the ascending numbers, feel or picture yourself floating upward very gently. In your mind, extend your hands high on either side of your body, moving them up and down, your arms changing to soft, feathery, glittering faery wings, scattering Tinkerbell gold flying dust. At the same time, visualise the sky enfolding you.

• You cannot fall. Remember, as Peter Pan says, it is all a matter of faith; enjoy the cool, rippling and free sensation of the air around you. The point when you let go of the earth and soar up toward the sun is the moment serious meditators call the "point of universal vision," where you can peer through a pinhole into the whole universe. When my son Jack was young, he called this "dancing the clouds."

• Slowly open your eyes, merging your physical vision with the sky and as the sky. Enjoy the flying sensation. When you are ready, close your eyes and count from thirteen down to one and float slowly downward.

• Eventually, you will no longer be aware of the point of the first jump, but your spirit body will effortlessly and instantaneously merge with the cosmos and your etheric fey self will fly wherever you want.

• In time, you can combine the visualisation part of the exercise with the physical shadow work, but with your eyes open. Do not force this stage. One day it will just happen, and the final step is to take away the shadow aspect and fly or float with the fey in your liberated mind anywhere, anytime.

• We will work much more with fey flight in the chapter on the air spirits and merging with the sylphs.

## Simulating Fey Flight

If the above techniques do not work for you, it does not mean you are doing anything wrong. It may be that you are a very logical, practical person, and it will take practice. The joys of this technique are worth persevering and the sensation will come if you relax and enjoy it.

Often physical flight will trigger the visualised flying experience initially. After that, your psyche will take over even in everyday situations.

Stimuli might include hang gliding, hot air ballooning, lying in a flotation tank, sky diving, bungee jumping, rock or mountain climbing, standing at the top of a tall building, riding in a cable car, or riding in a funicular railway. For example, at the top of the Auckland Sky Tower on New Zealand's North Island, it is possible to step on a glass floor and see the world spinning directly far below.

Alternatively, journeys by plane are an excellent opportunity to perfect astral travel, especially as the aircraft is rising off the tarmac and you project yourself into the fluffy white clouds at the point of takeoff (excellent for calming flight nerves). On a clear day, use the midair cloud and shadow formations beneath you. You will see the air spirits sitting on the clouds.

In the next chapter, we will work with the spirits of your locality.

Chapter 1 Sources

1. Frazer, James George. *The Golden Bough: A Study in Magick and Religion*. Charleston: Forgotten Books, 2008.

2. Kane, Tracy. *Fairy Houses* (The Fairy Houses Series). Lee, NH: Light Beams Publishing, 2001.

3. Barrie, J. M. *The Little White Bird; or, Adventures in Kensington Gardens*. New York: Hard Press, 2006.

4. Eason, Cassandra. *Psychic Power of Children: And How to Deal with It*. Slough, UK: Quantum/Foulsham, 2005.

# 2

## IDENTIFYING YOUR
## LOCAL NATURE SPIRITS

Nature spirits exist everywhere in the world. We can work with spirits from any lands who offer the powers we need, regardless of where we are living.

The spirits that best assist us magically and with whom we will be most instantly in tune are those indigenous to the region in which we currently reside. This is because we can tune in directly to their energies. We also have natural kinship with fey beings from our root culture through our family ancestry. Furthermore, if you live in an area where many people from the same country have resettled, you will also feel the influences of the faeries from their original homelands. For example, in Australia and the American continent, many fey people came with the settlers from Eastern and Western Europe, the Baltic, Scandinavia, and Asia and have sometimes made an uneasy truce with the original nature being inhabitants.

Too often, we dismiss the local fey in favour of the exotic. We know it is best health-wise to eat local produce in season and indeed to offer this to your local nature spirits who will take the essence and share the rest with the wild animals. So too, a ritual in situ using local herbs, seeds, and plants will fill your nature spirit ceremonies with a rootedness the exotic fey magick sometimes lacks, especially if you are casting a water or air spirit spell.

Try the following two nature spirit seed rituals rather than take my word. Though the rituals will work with any dried seeds, it is even more effective with ones produced close to home.

## A Seed Transformation Rite when Life Is Too Much

This rite helps when people or situations are very difficult and you can do no more to appease them.

- Take a dish of seeds to your garden or your nearest open space. Hold your dish upward to the sky and say, "Spirits of this land, I ask you to relieve me of this burden, worry, or distress."

- Name your burdens in as much or little detail as you wish. If you speak aloud, the words will stir the energies and rebound as positive power to free you from the restrictions weighing you down.

- Now hold the dish downward over the earth close to a tree, bush, or over a patch of growing flowers or greenery and say, "You Spirits of this land, I have done my best. I leave all in your hands."

- Scatter your seeds to grow, lie fallow, or wither.

## Bird Spirit Seed Wishes for Peace

Birds are traditional messengers that carry wishes to the cosmos. They are close companions of air spirits and the bird's form is often taken by air spirits. What is more, birds and animals have acted as omens for nature spirit messages for thousands of years. Wild birds confirm decisions regarding your worries by appearing in an unexpected location or coming unusually close. Often, these birds are nature spirits communicating with you.

The blackbird, that in the Celtic Otherworld myths becomes a rainbow bird, says, *Hey, be brave and you will shine*. Persistent Grandfather Crow, traditional messenger of the Native American and Norse world, asks, *How many warnings do you need? Stop, be still, listen, observe, and the answers are in nature for you.*

You too can use the air spirits in bird form to carry wishes for peace and harmony in a troubled world.

- Hold a container of birdseed, face each of the four directions, and say this adapted version of the Druid prayer I use when working with my local air spirits on the Isle of Wight, a small, semirural island off the south coast of England: "May there be peace in the north, peace in the east, peace in the south, and peace in the west. You spirits of the air, carry from this land peace throughout the whole world."

- If you wish, add, "and may there be peace within me," for if we are not at peace with ourselves, how can we bring harmony to others?

- Feed the birds with the seeds.

## Rediscovering Local Fey Legends

Though the vast majority of formal research on faery beings has been recorded in Celtic, European, and Scandinavian countries, there will be nature spirits indigenous to the land wherever you live, even in a city. These indigenous nature spirits have been in the area for hundreds or even thousands of years. They have old stories about their origins and characteristics that reflect the terrain, and these secrets can be discovered by talking to locals or searching guide books for legends.

If you do live in or spend time in a country where nature still runs free, such as the vast tracts of the Australian outback or the open plains of the United States, indigenous spirits will still be a major focus. As such, regardless of your own land ancestry, it is vital you understand, respect, and work with these rooted local energies.

I have used a number of examples from France because this is an area where I have stayed and researched extensively for twenty-five years, beginning when my now-grown children were tiny and ran with the faeries. France is, along with Ireland, probably the richest source of recorded fey myth.

## Rock Spirit Myths

Local legends on nature spirits are frequently focused around names such as "Giant's Rock" or the "Hill of the Faeries." Some fey stories are hidden behind Christian myths; often, locals will know of these older versions, so take time to talk in the cafés and bars. For example, there are a number of *La Rigole du Diable,* which means "the trough of the devil," giant rock formations in central France. Though they are natural, the rocks may be in a relatively flat landscape and so are believed to have been hurled by an angry giant or demonic nature spirit. I have written about nasty nature spirits in chapter 9. Look closely at the rocks and you will see natural sculptures of the ancient guardian spirits who manifest in their rocks.

For example, the huge rock formation I visited at Royère de Vassivière in the Limousin region of La Creuse in France was, according to Christian accounts, the site where the local parish priest Camille was threatened that the devil's gargoyles and little red devils would cause huge rocks and water to fall, blocking the valley of Thaurian. Camille managed to defeat the devil by getting his cockerel to crow before the devil's, so the road is clear except for the odd passing tractor.[1]

There is a very clear, apparently demonic face naturally etched in the huge granite rocks, and the Christian devil is based on the ancient antlered animal spirits who were once worshipped as deities. A saint or priest is usually credited with overcoming evil forces and bad luck at one of these powerful sites, especially in a land such France where organised religion is very dominant. The French Christian legend may have been a way of explaining the natural rock sculpture of a rock guardian and next to it what appears to be a hooded man or woman in the rocks, possibly Camille or in the older tradition a second guardian of the place. Both figures are entirely untouched by human hand. In pre-Christian times, offerings were left for the guardians by locals at seasonal change points and the sites of ceremonies—the very same rock formations in the Christian legends. The offerings were left to ensure that the powerful rock guardian spirit granted their blessings on crops and cattle.

In some rural places, the fey associations have survived unaltered. At Saint-Yrieix-les-Bois, not far from Peyrabout in the Limousin region of La Creuse in Central France, the village of Beaumont is dominated by a hill whose summit is crowned by a natural pile of rocks, called locally the "Castle of the Faeries." Here are rock pools where tributes have been left to the fey from time immemorial. At the foot of the hill in Beaumont village square is a fountain. When the vapours rising from the fountain appear above the trees, people say the faeries are doing their laundry. *Peyrabout* means "standing stones," and megaliths were traditionally built along ley lines that are associated with frequent nature spirit appearances.[2]

## Reawakening and Recording the Old Legends

In the modern, changing world, it is important to rediscover and record forgotten or overwritten nature essence legends, for they are etched in the land. All legends were created by people who tried to explain the energies of the spirits they detected in a place, but it is a dying art. One of the purposes of this book is to encourage you to psychically tune back into the stories of the land and its spirits and record them digitally for future generations.

This is especially important if your local fey-named places are built over with new development as has happened with many sacred springs and wells. If you are on holiday in a region you know and love well, you can link into their indigenous traditions using the same methods used for your home territory; for me, France is such a place.

# Pendulum Fey Legends

It is much easier to tune in to the nature spirit legends in a place that is unspoiled. However, always ask before taking a picture of a fey place or sitting and recreating the old stories. Sometimes the spirits may not want to be recorded. While walking in the woods near the devil's rocks described above, I was trying to take a picture of a lovely faery door in a rock about halfway up the rock formation at the side of the path. Suddenly, a stick flew upwards from the ground, smacked my camera arm and rather less poetically my bra twanged and unfastened. I did not take the picture.

Where legends are lost or never recorded, psychic recreation will bridge any gaps and open totally lost stories, stored in time warps. We all have the power of the storyteller within us, so trust yourself.

- Take a pendulum or use your hands and stand in a forest at the top of a hill or by rocks with a fey, religious, or mystical name.

- Stand near the rock face or perch near a particular natural stone etching; the features may not be so distinguishable up close. Otherwise, face a magnificent tree or the edge of a body of water or spring.

- Hold the pendulum in your dominant hand; if it is too windy, extend your hands so your palms are vertical, half an extended arm span from your body.

- Keep your fingers close together and slightly curved inwards to activate your palm and fingertip energy centres. Some people always prefer to use their hands. Either way, you are connecting your own aura or energy field with the energy field of the place that contains the energies of nature essences and old legends that have been woven around the place over time.

- Ask the guardian of the place that you may be given the fey story you are to pass on to future generations.

- You will feel a tingling in your hands or the pendulum will spiral as it is caught up in the flow of the time tunnel.

- You will hear in your mind or externally in bird calls or rustling leaves the overwhelming chatter, colours, and sounds as the events and essences of the place and human intervention caught up in the stories are released into your energy field.

- This is the same sensation you will experience when you are working with the nature essences of land where indigenous spirits mingle with a strong indigenous tradition (see later in this chapter).

- If you allow all these sensations to whirl and swirl around you, gradually one particular story or impression will predominate. Gradually you may hear a soft voice stilling the other sounds internal and external, telling you the story as though to a child. The voice belongs to the story keeper spirit of the place, as old as time, and she can be heard whenever you connect to ancient prerecorded or forgotten traditions.

- When the story ends, sit in a comfortable place and take up your fey journal. I will describe later in this chapter how to make your fey journal. Allow your hand to write or sketch images spontaneously. Even if you are not normally a writer or artist, the inspiration will flow very naturally. When you are finished, close your book and thank the story keeper and the guardians of the place.

- Before you leave, take some digital camera images, especially those that capture faces and figures in trees or stones.

- Try to pass on the legends within your family and friends and online, or collect together a new book of local legends including ones that are already known. We are the storytellers of tomorrow.

# Working with Indigenous Nature Spirits in Situ

Some spirits are naturally rooted in the land and have been so for thousands of years, but they will relate with and even assist respectful visitors or those who have settled on the land.

Take the *Mimi*, or *Mimih*, rock spirits who have been recorded in early Australian Aboriginal rock-shelter art. These rock spirits are said to be older than the art, which itself dates back forty thousand years. Mimi are accepted by the Aboriginal people as totally natural and as objectively real as humans. For central to Aboriginal spirituality is the interconnectedness of all life and the spiritual and material worlds are one and the same. If a tree is cut down, the man or woman shares its pain.

Though Mimi are portrayed in and associated with the rocky escarpments of western Arnhem Land and are described in the folklore of the indigenous people of northern Australia they have been seen all over this vast continent. Mimi are described as living in family groups, having extremely thin and elongated bodies, and are naked with big heads and hair. They usually spend most of their time living in rock crevices. They are said to have taught the early people how to hunt, prepare kangaroo meat for food, and use fire.

Mimi resemble small imps. Because they are so fragile, they rarely go out if it is windy. Generally shy of humans, they will hide in rock crevices or if there are no suitable hiding places they have the power to open rocks and seal them once inside. However, though tiny, Mimi can be perceived as larger and have been helpful to people in distress. In the previous chapter, I described how when Gary was twenty-four he was missing in the outback for eleven days and the little brown beings ran about him chasing the bark and tucking the pieces all about him to keep him warm until he was found.

## African Spirits Who Traveled to the Americas

*Simbi*, Central African water spirits, were first reported in the South Carolina low country by a geologist in search of marl deposits in 1843.[3] They were associated with the hardships of African slaves who were illegally transported from ports in West Central Africa to the plantations, a trade that began over one hundred years earlier. Simbi spirits were both feared and regarded as protectors of the people they accompanied from Africa. They came with the slaves as guardians of the local American water springs. Because one in three slave children died before their sixteenth birthday, many as small infants, the people certainly needed protection. A story is told of an unnamed elderly slave who persuaded a planter not to enclose a spring for fear of angering the Simbi spirits. *Bisimbi* (the plural of Simbi), the term used among the original African *Kikongo* speakers, are called *cymbees* in Carolina and have survived in modern folklore, especially among those of African descent.

It was believed if the Simbi spirits were offended, the springs would dry up. In earlier times in Africa, they brought good hunting as well as harvests and this belief was transferred to the slaves' small Sunday gardens and their hunting of small animals and birds, as this helped them to not starve. However, in a more sinister way, Simbi spirits were blamed for the disappearance of young women who went to fetch water, and for children drowning. If angered, they could also stir up high winds. Shrines to them were set up at the springs and rituals followed by the African people to ensure their positive blessings. The Simbi spirits were described as humanlike, each with unique features, according to the water source.

Das Michael Brown, a researcher at Dillard University in New Orleans, has studied Simbi spirits extensively.[4] He reports that "connections made by West-Central Africans of ancestors with nature spirits suggest that territorial deities represented elders of the Other World. Their presence allowed those who lacked ties with named ancestors or who may have come to a region as strangers to still have access to agents of Other Worldly powers and to feel attached to the land (South Carolina) where they (now) lived."

## Indigenous American Spirits

There are numerous indigenous Native American spirits. Some, like the *Gans,* have passed into local hunting folklore of the settlers and travelers asked them for protection, though at first they were feared as demons. These mountain spirits of the Apache Indian nation are invoked in dance, song, and night rituals by their own people for safe journeys, good weather, luck, and protection from evil spirits. They guard the mountains of southwest North America. The Gans are traditionally considered important in Apache rituals for rites of passage, healing, and rain. Warriors imitate the spirits wearing body paint; tall, wooden, slat headdresses; and black masks specifically in the Crown Dance or Mountain Spirit Dance.

The *Nunnehi* fey people of old Cherokee County were said to be invisible unless they wanted to be seen, when they would take on an ordinary appearance. Great musicians and drummers, it is said to have been impossible to follow their sound which moves ever further away. They would rescue lost travelers and were believed to live in underground townhouses, marked on the surface by a hole like a chimney from which warm vapours would rise. Though many Nunnehi spirits traveled with the Native Americans on their eight-hundred-mile Trail of Tears to Oklahoma in 1835, others remained with the Cherokee people who hid in the hills and were later granted land in modern Cherokee county. Therefore, the Nunnehi also still protect their original homelands in North Carolina. It is said that if one were to find a lost tool or knife in this area, it is important to leave tobacco, beads, or another offering in exchange and ask permission to take the finding.

Other Native American spirits include the *Algonquian* star people who live in the sky and can cast spells on humans unless they are given offerings.

## Connecting with Indigenous and Migrant Nature Spirits in Situ

In the Treasury of Faery Wisdom in the appendix, I have described faery rings and other places traditionally associated with the fey. It is not generally considered wise to work within a circle of mushrooms or toadstools, though you can walk nine times around the outside and cast an offering into the centre while making a wish nine times.

Some areas are known for fey circles, for example the discs of completely bare sandy soil that vary in size from two to ten metres in diameter. These are found exclusively along the western coastal fringes of the Namib Desert in southern Africa. These are easily distinguishable because they are bare in the middle, yet have unusually lush perimeters of tall grasses which stand out from the otherwise sparse vegetation of the desert. These fey circles have defied scientific explanation.[5]

Generally, however, faery places tend to be a single clearing in woodland or a natural circle where there is only a little grass in an otherwise lush meadow. You will find your own naturally occurring faery places and may locate different ones in your vicinity when working with different kinds of faeries, for example a flat, grassed area on a rocky outcrop on a hillside for air spirits. In these faery spots, you will sense a number of different but related energies that suggest there is a fey community.

In time, you will discover one or two favourite locations close to home for your private meditations or rituals, but remember after any ritual you should always leave only your footprints and natural offerings.

## Discovering Your Personal Faery Name

In your own location, you can work with the indigenous fey as well as any fey associated with your root culture however distant back and those associated go. For example, the large number of Scottish and Irish people in West Virginia that have given rise to numerous banshee sightings (see chapter 4 for more on banshees).

Just as when you were recreating legends, at first you may have felt overwhelmed by impressions, colours and sounds, so as you tune into your local fey you may find the chattering of the different fey groups confusing, especially if indigenous and settler faeries are still squabbling over territory.

As you meditate or sit quietly on the ground in your chosen fey space, hold your pendulum or hold both palms downward. You may not only connect with the different fey nations, but on the first or second occasion you should be given your secret fey name by the ruling nature spirit of the place. This is the name by which they will call you.

The name you are given will suddenly come into your mind or you will hear it on the breeze. It can be used at the beginning of any fey magick ritual or empowerment. It might be the name of a flower, herb, tree, star, a favourite crystal or a mythical faery name, perhaps associated with one of the pre-Christian gods or goddesses.

Hayley, who lives in Buckinghamshire, not far from London, explained how she received her magical name. "I was following a guided meditation when I saw a little fey flitting with me throughout the journey. Toward the end she called me 'Clionda,' then there were three faeries and I was presented with a willow headpiece and wrapped in a silken cloth."

Clionda, a downsized-Celtic goddess, is the golden-haired faery queen of the seashore who still rules over every ninth wave. She is said to heal the sick with her magical birds (see chapter 4 for more of her story).

## A Meditation to Meet and Greet the Spirits of the Place

- Sit in a local place of beauty or quiet woodland on a calm day, early in the morning or in the early evening when even a city will be relatively quiet. Urban wildlife gardens are excellent for fey connection as are botanical gardens, not in an exotic part of the garden but one dedicated to local flora. At other times, botanical gardens and hothouses will also enable you to experience the fey of the lands of their origins, though of course your indigenous faeries will not let the incomers have it all their own way. If you do not already know the history of you area, research any major migrations into your area from overseas as well as your own ancestral roots if your family has not always lived in the same area.

- Find a comfortable seat and hold your pendulum in your dominant hand.

- Hold your hands so the palms are facing downward and you feel comfortable and relaxed. You are using your pendulum or hands as an aerial to amplify the fey impressions.

- Close your eyes and breathe very gently and slowly through your nose and out again so that one breath follows another in an unbroken stream.

- Visualise two beautiful, shimmering faeries resting, one on each foot, small as butterflies with translucent wings.

- Hold your feet as still as you can. Gently inhale; as the faeries rise, relax and exhale.

- See the faeries next on your knees. Again, hold your knees motionless so as not to disturb them as you breath. Exhale gently and slowly as they are in the air again.

- Continue as they land together on your navel, then separately on your hands, separately on each breast, together on the throat, separately on each shoulder, together at the top of the spine, and finally side by side on the crown of your head.

- Allow them to move down again stage by stage to your feet and finally to fly off.

- Half open your eyes slowly. Put your free hand as a cup around the pendulum so that it is not quite touching but encloses the pendulum. Alternatively bring your hands close together so the palms are facing each other, vertically inwards close to your lap, in a prayer position, but not touching.

- Move your hands slowly to and fro so they almost touch to build up the energies between them.

- Close your eyes once more. Focus on the actual place you are sitting, but ask to be shown the land as it was long ago. Allow a picture to come spontaneously to tune into the original land spirits. You may be surprised, as it could once have been covered in water or a dense forest.

- Wait without expectation and indigenous nature beings will fly, run, or perhaps float towards you.

- Do not force the impressions, but greet the original spirits of the land and ask them to bless you. Promise you will always do your best to respect the land and create beauty.

- When they fade, move forward in your mind, counting slowly one hundred years at a time. You will see other spirits perhaps belonging to different settlers, one following another effortlessly on your part.

- Again, greet each new spirit or groups of spirits, ask for blessings, and promise to respect the land.

- If your own ancestors came to the land generations ago, you will likely connect with their spirits during your meditation. If you are the first to move here from another region, ask your own spirit guardians of your homeland to reveal themselves last of all and again ask for blessings and promise to preserve the heritage.

- With your eyes still closed, say, "I return to the present. Show me yourselves, wise spirits of the past who still are here and ever will be."

- Now you will become aware of all the different generations and nations of fey people who coexist in an area; you will probably be surprised about how many there are.

- Just one fey will move forward, the fey person with whom you have most affinity. This fey person could be an indigenous spirit or one from your root culture. You can always call this particular spirit while you are in the area. The spirit may reveal their name or you may just know it instinctively. To your surprise, it may be the guide who appeared in the meditation when you first visited faeryland in chapter 1.

- Your spirit may call you by your new, secret name you discovered in the previous exercise and he or she may have a message for you. Afterward, thank your special spirit and the guardians of the place.

- Open your eyes slowly and you may still see the fey gathered around and your special guardian.

- Wait until they fade and record all you have seen and heard in your fey journal (see below) .

- As an offering, do something to improve the immediate location, for example removing choking weeds from a sapling, picking up litter, or clearing a blocked stream.

## Making and Keeping a Fey Journal

Your fey journal can be created in any form you wish, and it can be written in as extensively with as much or little detail as you choose. Some people record special nature spirit experiences on holiday and photographs of beautiful natural landscapes with fey associations. Others use it as an ongoing resource book with detailed lists of nature spirits and relevant herbs or flowers with which they are linked.

- Your fey journal can act as an ongoing diary of your discoveries and interactions with nature spirits throughout your lifetime. Begin with experiences with faeries or nature spirits from your childhood. If you have children or grandchildren, write down their magical sayings, dreams, and visions. Too often, the details become blurred in everyday living.

- One day, you may choose to pass on your book as a legacy to a special child, grandchild or friend, publish parts of it or deposit it in an archive to help future research into nature spirits and to help keep the old knowledge and ways alive.

- There is no substitute for a handwritten fey journal. Black ink on white or cream paper is customary, though you may prefer green ink. When outdoors, use a ballpoint pen, but a fountain pen is best for special work. You can sometimes buy plant-based inks.

- With a handwritten journal, sit among nature and record precious moments, fey experiences, and impressions in situ, perhaps adding pressed flowers or leaves from the fey site. Add a date and location, as it is all too easy to confuse sites particularly if you are sightseeing.

- Have a waterproof pouch for carrying your journal. Digital tablets, while convenient, are nowhere near as magical and you do not want emails bleeping through to irritate the faeries and spoil a moment.

- A loose-leaf version with separate sheets of paper that slip into a leather book cover is ideal. Date notebooks as they become full. List the contents and file safely. You have the option of copying the most relevant parts into a particularly beautiful blank-paged notebook with a faery or natural scene on the front.

- Illustrate your journal with drawings, paintings, and digital-camera images of magical places you visit; close-ups of fey flowers and crystals; as well as images of your fey indoor and outdoor place (see the Introduction) in moonlight, sunlight, and in different seasons.

- If you photograph a tree, you may notice a faery door or gnome recorded on the image afterward. Waterfalls may be dancing with water spirits not visible to the human eye.

- Keep an even smaller notebook with you for noting information about any unusual plants or herbs you see in a faery place whenever you have a day out, a weekend away, or holiday. Take pictures of them so you can identify them later.

- Scribble down legends of faery wells, ancient sites, local rhymes, chants, and any relevant information on sign boards. Take an image of the signs you see.

- Most significantly, spontaneously write your impressions of the fey spirits you encounter, drawing quick images and noting colours. A box of watercolour pencils is a useful tool.

- Though you may recognise many of the nature spirits from those described in this book, the way you perceive a spirit may be totally unique and equally as valid as what others have reported. This is because of the diversity of spirits and because each of us makes a unique connection between our aura energy field and theirs.

- If you relax and let your hand write without conscious thought, using a psychic process called automatic writing, you can intuitively rediscover the original spirit who inhabited the glade.

- All kinds of unexpected people come out with fascinating information or experiences in shops or cafés near a sacred site. It is all too easy to forget details and not be able to trace the source if we do not scribble it down as it comes; a mobile phone voice recorder may inhibit the story eller, especially someone from a traditional society.

- In addition, begin a cuttings folder for interesting articles, postcards, or small pamphlets from places you visit. Pamphlets in visitor centres or even churches are valuable sources of information. If you file them, you can translate them at a later date if need be.

- Note also the titles, authors, and page references in any books on faeries or legends you read if there are any new or exciting facts or theories.

- There are many books and leaflets being self-published, especially reprints of old books originally written in Victorian times when fey research was at its height. These are pure treasures. Look also in old bookshops near fey sites for tattered old copies with sepia images.

- Have a special section in your fey journal for the legends and messages psychically communicated to you, as well as any poetry you are inspired to write.

- Start a folder on your computer for your most significant fey findings; a digital archive will allow you to find information quickly, and notebooks can get lost or damaged. Information stored on computer has the benefit of being easily edited and rearranged. It is worth backing up your work on a memory stick or portable hard drive so that you can create a cyber treasury of fey wisdom over the years, in spite of computer crashes and losses.

- The Internet will also give you a valuable source of fey information worldwide and you can get basic translator programs to give you the gist of material in other languages.

- You can also access on line reference material such as www.sacred -texts.com or www.bl.uk/onlinegallery/sacredtexts/index.html and find copies of out-of-print books online as well as information on local forums studying nature and earth energies.

In the next chapter we will work with the fey people who protect your home and family.

Chapter 2 Sources

1. http://www.educreuse23.ac-limoges.fr/monteil/rigole
   /legende/cure/3.htm

2. http://www.france-voyage.com/towns/saint-yrieix-les
   -bois-5773.htm

3. Orr, Bruce and Kayla. *Ghosts of Berkeley County, South Carolina.*
   Charleston: History Press, 2011.

4. http://www.mamiwata.com/simbi.html

5. Fairy Circles:
   http://video.nationalgeographic.com/wallpaper/photography
   /photos/mysterious-earth/desert-fairy-circles/

# 3

WORKING MAGICALLY WITH
THE PROTECTORS OF YOUR
HOME AND WORKPLACE

There is a worldwide tradition of protective and usually helpful house elves or small nature spirits who share their home with humans. They care for their animals and any outbuildings and vehicles. In earlier times, when craftspeople worked from home (a trend increasing again in the modern technological world) the home spirits also protected the workshop in home. Now they guard home tools of trade (which in the modern world includes iPads, mobile phones, computers, and even games consoles, even though they do not understand them). If you get odd bleeps when you are asleep, your domestic spirits may be trying to fathom Facebook.

Many people in Scandinavia, Germany, the Netherlands, Eastern Europe, and Russia, especially in rural areas, still actively welcome these essences in their homes and workplaces. Those whose ancestors come from these lands have carried the tradition across the globe to countries where there are already existing nature spirits, and the different traditions may vie for supremacy. For example, according to an account by Mary, an Australian migrant from the

UK now living in Queensland, rugged settler faeries regularly engage in fierce battles with the indigenous darker-skinned Aboriginal nature spirits for dominance of her garden.

# Connecting with Domestic Spirits

Unlike nature spirits who live independently of and largely irrespectively of humans, home spirits connect with specific families and may indeed move home with their family. However, if a building is old or the land has a new or relatively new dwelling built on it, the spirits may be attached to that and remain when the current residents move on.

Many people regularly hear their house elves at night as well as sense or see their presence, sometimes all too clearly. Often when householders complain about ghostly activity downstairs, it is usually just the house elf tidying up or stumbling over soft-drink cans and potato-chip wrappings and grumbling and clattering a bit, just as we do when cleaning up after teenagers' untidiness.

A house where no one lives or a shop that often changes hands may have lost its resident guardian spirits, in which case there are ways of attracting them back that I will describe later in this chapter.

## House Elves and Pets

House elves love cats. It is said if you treat your cat well, the house elf will bring extra prosperity to your home. Occasionally, your house elf may shape shift into your cat's double, so you will see the cat sitting at the top of the stairs and suddenly he is by your side. Don't worry, for your house elf is just playing tricks.

### Asking Permission

Apparent poltergeist activity, with banging and crashing and breaking and moving items you know you left in a particular place, may occur because you haven't asked the permission of the house elf or elves before redecorating or making changes. Perhaps you forgot to inform your resident unseen old gentleman guardian that there is a new member of the family—or that you are going away for a while. Until the 1900s, people in many traditions would make domestic offerings when building a new house, maybe burying a shoe in the wall or a clay pipe behind the stove. These are occasionally unearthed when renovations take place. If you find one, put it back where you found it.

Does it sound strange asking permission of an invisible spirit to repaint your kitchen? Experiment with a couple of do-it-yourself projects, and ask permission in one and not the other. See which has the most mishaps.

## Russian House Elves

Though house elves are common to all cultures, we can discover most about them by studying cultures where their presence is well recorded. One of the best examples is the Russian and Eastern European family *domovik*, a male guardian spirit who lives under the doorstep or behind the stove.[1]

Russian *domovoi* (plural for domovik) are often described as hairy, gray, bearded gnomes. They are most often knee high, old, and benign. In Poland, however, the domovoi come to resemble the male head of their human family, living or dead. Other names for these spirits include the Bulgarian *stopan* and the Serbian *domani*.

The domovik is especially concerned with safety against domestic fires; his female companion is sometimes given the name of the old domestic goddess Kikimora and nags him incessantly. When a family moves to a new home, it is tradition to take fire from the old hearth to the new so that the domovik will also move with them.

Though domovoi especially protect their families against evil spirits and help around their homes, they may cause poltergeist activity when annoyed. It is also said domovoi may start small fires if their family really behaves badly. Domovoi act as the family oracle, howling to warn of coming trouble. Their laughter is a sign of good fortune; the sound of a tune being played on a comb heralds a wedding in the domovoi family.

It is traditional to wrap salted bread in a white cloth beneath the stove to please the domovik; old shoes hanging in the yard is another way of welcoming this house spirit.

## Bannik

Another Russian and Baltic spirit who protects the home is the *bannik*. The bannik lives in the steam of the sauna bath, but also appears under different names in other lands. The bannik communicates through touch, though he, like other washroom spirits, may be glimpsed through the vapour or as a misty reflection if you rub a steamy mirror. A gentle touch on your back indicates good fortune coming, while scratching on your back is a sign you should be extra careful in the twenty-four hours ahead.

## Tomte

Though Sweden is a modern technological society, the belief in the *tomte* (or plural *tomtar*) house elf is among the strongest in the modern world. This is true of families of Scandinavian descent throughout the world. The name means "homestead folk," though now the tomte is equally at home in high-rise Stockholm apartments.

A large number of logical, tech-savvy people to whom I have spoken in Sweden have reported glimpsing the household tomte as "a small, elderly male spirit who lives in the store cupboard, behind the stove, in stables, in barns, or in grain stores on the farm." He wears grey clothes and a red-knitted cap and usually sports a white beard.[2] Some claim to have a whole family of resident house elves or a husband and wife.

These very special beings are called *nisse* in Denmark, *tusse* or *haugbo* in Norway, *kobolds* in Germany, *haltari* in Finland, *brownies* in England and Scotland, and *bwcas* in Wales.

At one time, the tomte would expect his special rice porridge with a pat of butter on the top every Thursday evening, which was his rest day, but many people now only do this on Christmas Eve, the main holiday, when a bowl of rice, flavored with cinnamon and spices, is left as an offering in almost every household.

In an oft retold story with numerous versions, a farmer who lived in the Lakeland area of Central Sweden was in a hurry one Thursday evening and by mistake put the butter in the bottom of the bowl where the tomte could not see it.

In fury the tomte (remember nature spirits are easily angered) killed all the farmer's cattle and then carried on eating. When he discovered the butter at the bottom, the tomte was so sorry he called his cousins, the mighty *huldre*, or *huldra*, and they brought magical cattle to replace the dead ones. These cattle gave twice as much milk as the ordinary ones and never got sick, so the farmer was content. Of course that story was told not literally, but to emphasize the point you need to respect household elves.

Tomtar are expert fiddlers and you may hear faint music in the night when they get together with others on Halloween, May Eve, Midsummer, and Christmas Eve. Midsummer is usually June twenty-first or twenty-second in the Northern Hemisphere when the household elf will expect a small shiny gift, for these house elves exist in every country.

## Vetter

The very small folk in Scandinavia are called *vættr* or *vetter*. Though vetter is the generic or type name for Scandinavian spirits who attach themselves to houses or work places, the name refers more specifically to tiny benign earth spirits who live under houses. They can be mistaken for mice or even large insects scurrying around in basements. Sometimes you can buy tiny crystal vetter to set on your hearth to protect your home against accidents, fire, or storms. They are also good in protecting against subsidence. It is good sense to honour them with offerings. You can use any small, brown, patterned agate or jasper (three, five, seven, or nine) and place them close to the doorstep or in a pot of growing greenery near the front door. They will attract these tiny luck-bringing creatures to your home wherever you live in the world.

## Brownies

These are the household faeries in Scotland and England. Welsh brownies are known as the *bwbach* or *bwcas*. They have also been reported in Denmark, Canada, and the United States.

Brownies, so called because of their brown skin and clothing, complete household tasks left unfinished by mortals during the day, though they prefer

to work outdoors. They will assist with building work (only wooden structures), repair broken tools, and bring good fortune when they adopt a home.
Sometimes brownies live as part of an extended family and several may make
a home in a single human dwelling or farm. Brownies are fond of roosters and
may shape-shift into one.

Brownies never let themselves be seen and if anyone tries to spy on them
at night they go away and take the luck with them. Brownies appreciate small
gifts or food, but usually abandon the house if humans refer to these gifts as
payments or offer gifts of clothes (no matter how shabby the brownies' own
clothes are). Some Scandinavian house elves also will leave if given clothes, as
in the Brothers Grimm tale "The Elves and the Shoemaker."[3]

## Kobolds

In Germany, house elves are called *kobolds*. In past times, they would also
guard castles and fortifications. There is some documentary evidence of a
famous kobold named Heinzelman. He lived in the castle of Hudemuhler,
in Lunenburg. In Grimm's folklore collections made in the early 1800s,
accounts of this kobold came from a local religious minister. Heinzelman
would clean pots and pans and care for the castle and horses. In return he
had a room with a straw-plaited chair and bed and insisted on a daily dish
of sweetened milk with bread crumbs.[4]

Hodeken, another kobold, according to the Brothers Grimm, lived with
the Bishop of Hildesheim. Like Heinzelman he was good-natured and hard
working but would take violent revenge on those who offended him. For
example, when the head cook was unkind to him, Hodeken squeezed toads
all over the meat being roasted for the bishop's dinner. He then hurled the
offending cook into the moat, which delayed dinner even more. For this out-
burst and other acts of fury, the bishop decided to remove the kobold with a
full exorcism ceremony and he came no more. In a local variation of the tale I
heard from a German schoolteacher, Hodeken took the luck of the castle with
him. When the bishop tried to find him to restore his former good fortune
Hodeken had disappeared and the bishop lived unhappily thereafter.

# Attracting or Attracting Back House Elves

If you buy a house and it seems dark, cold, and unfriendly it may be that the house elf or elves left because the people were always quarrelling or simply did not recognise their presence. Household elves make any home feel lived in and alive. You'll know the difference if you go into a house where the vitality of the place is missing. If you have more than one elf, you will hear them chattering very softly when the house is quiet at night.

- If you want to attract a house elf back into your home, sit at the furthest edge from either your front or back door, on a balcony, or by an open window and whistle softly and slowly three times. If you can play pan pipes, make three rising notes or use a flute. Do this at sunset on six days (skip Thursday, the traditional day of rest for house elves).

- On a windy day, stand near the house and call a friendly elf into the wind.

- In the evenings play fiddle music on CD—they love it.

- Hang shiny crystals or old necklaces from trees as all house elves love shiny things.

- Use your faery house or faery door (see page 20) in the garden or house and on it tie an invitation to enter your home. Otherwise tie one to your bird house.

Skeptics will say this is superstitious, unscientific nonsense, but if you do attract a benign elf to your new or existing dwelling, watch your luck soar and the new wallpaper or paint stay on the wall.

# Offerings

Once you have a house elf in situ, ensure he stays happy.

- Thursday evening is best for offerings. There is an old superstition that on a Thursday evening you should not chop wood outside, or in

modern terms, fix the motor bike or carry out car repairs for fear
of offending the relaxing house elves with the noise.

- If your family luck has not been particularly good recently or there has
been a lot of clattering in the night, car keys getting lost, or electrical
items blowing fuses seemingly without reason, leave your household
elf or elves a tiny bowl of some sugared or honeyed white porridge or
pudding with cinnamon and a pat of butter on top every Thursday (any
rice pudding or oat porridge you make for the family is fine).

- Leave it in an outbuilding or put it by the hearth or in a corner of the
kitchen. A house elf only eats the essence and not the actual food. The
next morning, give it to an animal. Humans should not eat house elf
porridge as they take offence.

- House elves of all kinds love golden rutilated quartz called "faery gold"
placed in a little dish by the hearth or in the room where the family
relaxes. You can use gold; amber, red, and golden tiger's eye; brown,
yellow, and cream agates; or sodalite and black tourmaline crystals.

- Keep a little dish of shiny things, old earrings, and costume jewelry in
a dish near the hearth, as a house elf loves borrowing things. You will
find your jewelry and trinkets stop going missing once you do this.

- House elves are also fascinated by doll houses and miniature
furniture.

- House elves also like tobacco and tiny cups of whole milk, the
creamier the better, again on Thursday evenings. They are not
into healthy eating.

- Find a corner close to the hearth, or a quiet place where the family
relaxes, to sit and talk quietly to your house elf when everyone is
in bed, but not on Thursdays. Catch up with your family's news and
warn the elves in advance about any parties you are planning.

# Higher Household Guardians or House Wights

Household guardians are more highly evolved protective household spirits. Though they are acknowledged mostly throughout the Scandinavian, Germanic, Mediterranean, and eastern and western European regions, every home has one. They are like guardian angels of the home, but are very definitely nature beings rather than heavenly beings.

Household guardians are natural luck and abundance bringers and are good if you have children, elderly, or sick people at home. Unlike house elves, they do not perform practical tasks but bring peace and harmony to busy households, warmth and a sense of belonging to a single person, and reassurance and patience to any couple going through a difficult period.

You may be aware of your house wights already. Cats may show an affinity with them, as well as with house elves. There was once a belief that cats, especially tomcats, could offer a home in their bodies for these protective and kindly spirits. If your cat is unusually wise or protective and very gentle with the children, you may have one of these special animal house protectors.

You may sense your household guardian at night if you come home late and are fumbling for your keys in a deserted street. Equally you will be nurtured as you sit by the fireside late at night or are awake with a child in the small hours of the morning.

House guardians often choose a beautiful statue or an amethyst geode in which to settle. You may feel strong but very good energies coming from the statue and occasionally small beams of light.

# Traditional Ritual to Find and Dedicate a Guardian Stone

You can choose any special stone to act as a focus and home for your house wight.

- Choose a small, rounded rock about the size of a small fist from close to (but not actually from within) a sacred place, a sea shore, an old burial mound, a stone circle, an old abbey, or a monastery. This should be within a few miles of your home if possible.

- Pass your hands, palms down and flat, a few centimetres above the top of the stone nine times. Move your right hand clockwise and at the same time move the left hand counterclockwise in the old magical, nature-spirit method called "enchantment" or "psychic empowerment".

- Maintain a slow, regular rhythm, saying softly and gently nine times "Be as guardian for me against all hostility and negativity. Let only harmony enter my beloved home. I thank you for your presence."

- Keep the stone by your hearth or the centre of your home for a year and a day, then return it to its former home and select a new guardian rock.

- Alternatively, you could buy a crystal geode, the kind with hollow rock like a doorway with tiny amethysts inside, again set near the centre of your home or on your hearth or close to the stove or fireplace and empower it in the same way. This you need not replace but rededicate it as you would the new guardian rock exactly as before.

- Each week, sprinkle a circle of water droplets in which you have dissolved a pinch of sea salt around your rock and ask for the blessings and protection and for the house wight to remain within your home. As with your house elves, mention any special plans, expected visitors, or unusual activities in the following week.

# Family Spirit Guardians

In terms of household spirit hierarchies, family guardians are the most evolved household spirits, traditionally associated with a family clan that is still spiritually and emotionally rooted in its history. This applies even if geographically the family has crossed the world to resettle, as guardians move home with the family and remain with different generations. They are nature spirits of a higher order, ranking between angels and general nature beings. They are almost always female and maternal.

Family guardians may also come to a couple starting their own family far away from home or who may have become severed from birth family roots because of adoption or some break in the family through death or the desertion of a parent. You may have deceased relatives protecting you and your family, but theirs are personal energies and they resemble you and will be with particular children. Nature guardian spirits are more generic and follow a fey type rather than displaying specific family characteristics, though they are emotionally attached to your family and may have been for generations.

## Bean Tighe

The *Bean Tighes*, or faery housekeepers, are known to reside in Ireland and Scotland and with families of Scottish or Irish descent in different parts of the world. There are other cultures who also have these faery godmothers with them, for though they are documented in specific cultures they are found in the oral traditions of many lands.

Bean Tighe means "woman of the house." She guards children and pets, especially during the night and helps exhausted mothers with unfinished household chores.

I heard a case of removal men asking "What happened to the old lady?" as they are unloading furniture in a new house, only to find out there was no old lady in the house—or at least no human old lady. Some are practical in their help while others are more protecting or guiding. If you want one of these spirits, bake bread and put fragrant flowers around the home to call them (see below for more suggestions).

## Duende

In Spain and Central and South America, the faery housekeepers are called *duendes*. They are mostly gossipy, middle-aged faery women dressed in green. Male duendes are found mainly in Spain; they are more benign and resemble frail old men with tall brimless hats. Duendes attach themselves to households. Unlike the Bean Tighe, the female duendes can be jealous of the mother or women of the home. The duendes clean because they hate messy homes, but sometimes throw crockery, move furniture, and hide possessions if annoyed by noisy children or animals.

Though duendes are traditionally said to have originally been fallen angels condemned to serving humankind as punishment for their pride for challenging God, they nevertheless display the fey trickster attitude. At markets, they pay with faery gold coins that resemble ordinary coins which disappear or turn into dust after they have left with the goods.

## Dísir

The *Dísir* (*Dís* plural) are, in the Scandinavian and Germanic traditions, spirit ancestral mothers of a specific family. They are not ghosts, but spirits who choose to become and remain part of the natural world in order to protect their family through the generations. In this sense, they are closer to spirit guides. Houses often have just one guardian mother. If your own mother is deceased or far away, these are wonderful guardian spirits with whom to connect simply by lighting a white candle each Friday evening, the day of the old Mother Goddesses and the Virgin Mary. While doing so, ask for protection and their ongoing presence.

Your own special Dís will draw close and protect your home and family and comfort you if you are sad. They are particularly powerful on Christmas Eve, called *Modranicht*, the night of the Mothers in the Anglo-Saxon tradition. Those who connect with the older seasons may, if they live in the Southern Hemisphere, feel them most strongly on the Midwinter Solstice that falls around June twenty-first.

If you are the mother of the house try to take five minutes out of the Yule celebrations regardless of where you live, to sit quietly and connect with the ancestral spirit mother.

## Kinfetch

*Kinfetch* are akin to Dísir and are female spirits who carry the luck and power of a family or a clan. The Kinfetch oversees the entire family far and near, wherever they are in the world, and ensure they think of home. Traditionally, they particularly protect the person seen as the head of the family, which means the person who cares for everyone else in the family.

## Banshee or Bean Sidhe

The banshee is part of a very old tradition, rooted in the belief that the Great Mother, sometimes in the form of the Moon Mother, absorbed and comforted the souls of the departed to await rebirth. The banshee is found traditionally in the fey lore of Scotland, Ireland, and Germany, but also there is a strong tradition of banshees in America where Celtic families have settled. The American author Susan Shepphard has extensively researched the banshee and says that the tradition is especially strong in West Virginia where she estimates 85 percent of families are with Scottish and Irish descent.[5]

One account she researched is of a banshee who traveled from the Marr Forest, north of Aberdeen, to the Mid-Ohio Valley with Thomas Marr and his family. Marr moved to Marrtown in 1836; after the Civil War, he obtained a job working as a night watchman at the toll bridge. Almost every night, Thomas saw a robed and hooded figure on a white horse as he traveled to and from his work that would disappear as he approached it. In February, 1874, Marr's wife Mary had been woken by sounds of footsteps. Outside the gate was a white horse whose rider wore a ragged veil. The rider told Mary that Thomas was dead. The shrouded woman and horse vanished as they reached the bend.

Within an hour the bad news was confirmed by one of Thomas's coworkers. Some claim that it was the cry of the banshee lamenting his demise that caused Thomas to fall into the water, but the banshee was never malicious and it is almost always the family of the departing person who hears the call. Indeed the banshee's role is to ease the passing. The banshee appeared at other family deaths and accidents including Mary's own death.

Traditionally, the banshee was recorded in five major Irish families: the O'Neills, the O'Briens, the O'Connors, the O'Gradys, and the Kavanaghs, but they are very common in other Celtic families whom have kept the family traditions alive. The banshee has been described as appearing as a young woman, a stately middle-aged woman, or an old hag.

The banshee is a folk version of the *Morrigu*, three Celtic sisters of battle, prophecy, war, and death; they are named Badhbh, Macha, and Mor-Rioghain. The banshee has also been described in the form of a hooded crow, stoat, hare, and weasel lingering outside the home. It may be that these Celtic deities were actually always higher nature spirits, for they are associated with trees or natural places such as deep, still pools.

In earlier times, the banshee assisted with birth, welcoming the new child to life and offering protection from danger as the child grew; then, when the same child had grown to be elderly, the banshee eased the passing at the end of life. There is another legend collected in the early 1900s; it tells that not long after the heir of the Scottish clan Macleod was born, a beautiful woman in wonderful clothes, described as a faery woman or banshee, went to the cradle of the new baby boy. She picked up the baby and sang a wonderful melody. This song foretold not only the life of the child but promised he would always be safe. Then the woman disappeared. As a result, the nurse of the heir in future generations sang the same magical verses to the child and part of the song is still part of the family heritage.[6]

## Making a Guardian Spirit Place

Set a special table to welcome your special higher natural protector in the heart of the home, such as the kitchen or a room where you relax. Cover the table with a white cloth. On it, place:

- A fossil or two to connect with past worlds and ancient wisdom that calls and offers a haven for traditional guardian spirits of your family, especially if you live in a new apartment or are far from home.

- An amethyst geode or amethyst crystal to connect with earth-spirit energies and purify the home from blocked energies and free-floating hyperactivity or negativity that may enter within the energy field of family members or your own aura after a stressful day.

- Photographs of your personal family ancestors, grandparents, and so on, whom the higher guardians once protected. This is very integrating if your family members are widely scattered or there have been estrangements.

- Fresh flowers or a green plant for any passing earth or air spirits to rest.

Encourage family members, young and old, to occasionally sit near the place by fire or candlelight and talk to them about the family history and events the future. If you live alone, write some of the old family stories for future generations as you sit in the place of the ancestors. The events of today are the family history of tomorrow, and we all too often forget in the frantic pace of daily life.

## Calling on the Protection of Your Household Guardians after Dark

The world is becoming increasingly dangerous; even in suburban areas, there are break-ins and vandalism, especially after dark. If you are afraid at night if you live alone, or if there are any particular threats such as gangs roaming outside your home, try this method weekly on a Sunday evening. This will activate the home or land spirit who lives in the guardian stone and your ancestral spirit.

- As darkness falls, light two white candles, one from the other.

• Name one candle for the house guardian and the other for the family guardian mother. Give each a private name only you know and use in ritual.

• Let the candles face an uncurtained window that does not have a streetlight directly outside, so that when you light the candles you can see the flames reflected in the window. If you have no such window, place the candles so they are reflected in a mirror.

• Say as you light each candle, "I call upon [name the guardian] to protect me through the night. Turn back any who would do harm, so all is calm till day returns as light."

• Now put salt, just a pinch, in each flame and say, "Blessings be on my home and on all those within my heart."

• Recite three times softly as you look into the flames,
   *"As the sun sets, power of dark,*
   *Kindle this protective spark.*
   *Weave your web of dark and light,*
   *Guardian spirits of the night."*

• Blow out the first candle just before you go to bed and carry the second still burning to your bedroom. Blow this one out just before sleep, saying, "May the light surround me and keep me safe until morning."

• Replace the candles regularly, but keep the same names.

If your area is particularly hazardous, after you have extinguished the first two candles, add a third white candle for the guardian of the area, traditionally called the Land Wight. Give this guardian a secret name you do not speak and say, "Roam far and near, turn back the phantoms of the night and fear, so all is calm till day return."

# Business Elves and Guardians

Work premises also have their helper spirits who may be most easily felt in an older building, especially if it has previously been used for industry, like a warehouse, old hotel, inn, or school.

Many years ago, when everybody worked from their homes or on local farms, house elves naturally lived and helped in barns, animal stores, and workshops. In town, they would find a comfortable place in the storeroom of shops and workshops behind boxes or on sacks in mills.

Wherever you work, even if it is a relatively new complex, you will almost certainly have elves that you may occasionally see out of the corner of your eye as you are opening up or closing for the day. These can be mistaken for store-room ghosts, but have a warm, light energy that you can feel darting around.

These workplace spirits should be well treated and thanked regularly, for they will attract a great deal of prosperity both to a company and those who work there. You can leave little crystals, small wooden or metal charms, or tiny, shiny pieces of jewelry in an open box in the storeroom.

Business elf crystals include amber, red and golden-brown tiger's eye, citrine (called the merchant's crystal), yellow-patterned or plain jasper, opal, and titanium aura.

# Encouraging Business Elves

If you take over a business where people don't stay long in the premises, the business may not have a store elf, as the elf may have been offended and left with the luck. A brand-new business or building will also need to attract its own business elf. You can attract one quite easily; there tend to be quite a few residing in business districts or where there are a number of shops.

- To attract a business elf, set a small ceramic gnome or elf figure in a window facing towards the street. It can be quite subtle, half-hidden in a display. Then hide clear quartz, citrine, amber, or tiger's eye crystals in plant pots or behind furniture as though you were indicating a pathway into the shop or premises for the elf. Pointed quartz crystals can be especially effective with points extending inward.

• Put a citrine crystal in any cash register and also one in a storeroom. They need not be on show for humans. This will attract a curious elf who will bring business with him.

• Place a soft, plaid blanket in the storeroom behind boxes, which should invite a house elf or maybe more than one to takes up residence. Before long, you will notice customers come earlier, phones ring with orders as you arrive, and business picks up.

• Should you work for a large impersonal firm, keep a little dish of fey crystals on your desk to improve your own career prospects.

• Place a little, wooden box in a high place on the premises and add an item weekly, but do not keep peering in to check what is going in and out. Empty it just before the Christmas break and leave a small dish of shiny, wrapped candy.

• A lot of so-called noisy ghosts in business premises are in fact work elves who have not been kept updated. When you first move to new premises, ask permission of the resident elves and explain what you will be doing; it saves a lot of crashing and banging about. After all, it is their home and may have been for generations if there have been businesses in the area for a long time.

• If you are the owner, tell the elves if anyone is leaving and who is replacing them. If you start a new job as an employee, visit the storeroom or a quiet place and introduce yourself and you will find that things go well for you.

• If you have a business problem, whether you are the owner or employee, tell the elves about it and leave a little shiny gift or crystal in a corner. Then forget it. By the next morning, an answer or unexpected opportunity will come, usually a solution through your own efforts but one you would not normally have thought of.

• If you work from home, you can adapt the above suggestions to attract a work elf if you use a special area of a room for the elf.

# Happy Stayday

Employees who fear a ghost's presence at hotels, bars, and restaurants may in fact be sensing a nature spirit who lives in the wine or beer cellar. Once these are acknowledged, spills become less and business improves.

## The Clurichaun

The *clurichaun* is a form of Irish leprechaun, but you may encounter one wherever you stay in the world. Often, you get different kinds of hotel and motel spirits who may move items and then return them, usually to the place you thought you left them but checked a dozen times.

The true clurichaun breed who lives in the cellar of pubs and hotels is invariably drunk, well dressed, and often has a red plant hat as a reminder he is a nature spirit. He has been described as having silver-buckled shoes, a white shirt, apron, and a red cap. A distinct asset in the cellar, the clurichaun prevents leaking casks or wine souring and acts as a protective spirit against unwelcome or unruly clients. He turns up in Australia, New Zealand, the United States, and Canada, especially in Irish pubs. He may be heard melodiously singing Irish folk songs, like all fey folk. He may ride the premises' watchdog, especially during full moonlight, but he does like a small tot of whisky left out nightly or he may sour the wine.

## Domestic Hindrance Spirits

Because home and business spirits are primarily wild, they should not be taken for granted, nor should they be regarded as wish supermarkets like the Disney faery godmothers.

Some domestic spirits do have a natural tendency toward mischief, but any can turn nasty if angered by people in the household or unruly animals or pets. *Boggarts* are ragged, dark house spirits who live in the north of England. They are covered with dark hair.

Boggarts are usually brownies who have been angered by an ungrateful adopted family and taken on a darker aspect. Often mistaken for a ghost, a furious boggart can shake curtains, make doors bang open and close, steal bread and butter (his favourite food) from children's hands to make them cry, hide tools, or cause china to shatter.[7] I came across several versions of almost identical stories in the folklore of Yorkshire in North East England and Denmark.

It is told that one particular Yorkshire boggart lived on a small farm in the early 1800s when such incidents were still being anecdotally recorded. The farmer became so tired of his boggart crashing around that he packed all his belongings and tied the family cows to the back of the cart ready to move south. Abraham, a neighbour, arrived and asked what he was doing. The farmer explained he was moving away from all the disruption in his home. At that moment a voice came from the butter churn on the cart: *Yes, Abraham, we can't stand the racket any longer so we're on our way.*

The farmer realised the boggart was moving with them and so returned home—and the family lived in peace ever after.[8]

## Moving Troublesome Spirits On

It is almost unheard of that you will need an exorcism for a domestic nature spirit because they are not usually evil, just bad-tempered. Bribery works wonders, especially shiny objects.

If you have a difficult resident spirit, you may have to sit down when the house is quiet and explain to the house elf that there is a problem, thank them for their presence, and apologise if you or a family member has accidentally caused offence.

Leave out some beer on the hearth on Thursdays in addition to extra porridge.

If you do have an uncooperative boggart and persuasion fails, trick him into leaving your home by asking him to stay away as long as the holly is green. He can never return. In tropical climates, choose an evergreen tough plant and bind the boggart in the same way.

## Children's Fears

Children often fear nature spirits after dark or if one peers in through the window. Nicholas was four years old and living in Norkopping in the Lakeland area of Central Sweden. The house had low windows and a porch at the back. Anne-Sophie, Nicholas's mother, told me there was a row of teddy bears along the window ledge. Suddenly Nicholas said, "Mama, stop that old man looking in at me. I want him to go away."

Nicholas described the figure as wearing a long grey cap, with a white beard, an old face, bushy eyebrows like his grandpa's and with wrinkled hands. From the description, the nature being was about the size of a small sturdy child, about adult-knee height. Ann-Sophie could not see the spirit, but very sensibly told him to go away, which he did, according to Nicholas. Nicholas would not talk about the experience for a long time, though he recalled it when I met his family when he was twelve years of age.

- With a child's natural psychic powers and vivid imagination, a mischievous spirit or two can make them afraid to sleep even in modern, urban apartments.

- If your child is afraid of a nature spirit, spend some time talking in daylight with him or her about the different sounds of the night—pipes clanking, owls hooting, distant traffic—and how shadows can seem to make faces, but really are just night pictures.

- Explain how you can make sure that, whatever is worrying them, together you can take it away by calling on the family angels and guardians.

- Before bedtime, switch off all lights except
a small lamp and recite faster and faster:
*"From ghouls and ghosties and long-legged beasties*
*From scaries and hairies and bad-tempered faeries*
*Kind angels protect us."*

- Encourage the child to join in clapping and add his or her special
fears—creaking floorboards, the branches of a tree banging
against a window, etc. It does not matter how long the list is.

- When the child is in bed, recite the rhyme six more times, making
each slower and slower and the clapping slower and quieter until
you and the child end in silence and stillness.

- Once your child is settled in bed, switch off the lamp, leaving maybe
an electrical night-plug glowing or a landing light switched on for
reassurance.

- Give your child an amethyst crystal by the bed. If the child wakes in
the night, tell him or her to hold the amethyst and the angels will take
away anything that frightens them, whether noisy central heating, a
noisy house elf, or a bird flapping outside the window.

## Protective Household Spirits Who Guard Property Against Intruders

Sometimes a spirit is not being nasty at all, just protecting *his* territory. About
eight years ago when I was lecturing at a festival in Malmo in Southern Sweden, I met a forty-year-old woman named Lotte who told me that her mother,
Sophia, lived alone near a forest in the countryside in the Lakelands of Sweden. Sophia insisted that she didn't need to move to be near the family because
she had her tomte to care for her and the home.

Sophia had gone to Spain for a few weeks with her sister to escape the
cold winter and one day received a frantic phone call from her other sister
in northern Sweden to say that their great nephew, Claude, a young man in

his early twenties, had been traveling and decided to get a bed for the night at his great aunt Sophia's. Typically he had assumed she would be there and did not phone ahead.

Finding the house empty, Claude thought she would soon be returning and decided to climb in through a half-open high window and find something to eat.

As he started to climb the ladder his great aunt had forgetfully left at the back of the house, his leg was grabbed by what seemed like a strong arm and he was pulled down and rolled on the ground.

When he looked up no one was there and there were no footprints in the snow. As Claude ran towards his car, terrified, he could hear heavy breathing and someone chasing him. Just for a second, he had a flash of a small old man, about four feet high, with a long, white beard shaking his fist and moving at great speed for a man of his apparent age.

Claude's car roared off skidding, and he could see no one in the rearview mirror. Being very scientific and sceptical, the young man turned the car around and decided to investigate, but he found he just could not get the tall gate to the house open again.

Claude did not want to call the police in case he was accused of trying to break in.

Lotte's mother roared with laughter when she heard about her "mad old gardener," as her sister called the guardian. Lotte's mother said, "I asked the Little People not to let anyone in 'till I returned, and they took me at my word."

Sophia said she often found that logs had been dragged up to the door when her fire supply was getting low, though there was no one for miles, but she did not talk about her tomte except to her daughter Lotte, as most of her family would think she was odd.

In the next chapter, we will work with the traditional faeries whose lore has most shaped the way we perceive the fey folk in modern culture.

Chapter 3 Sources

1. http://en.wikipedia.org/wiki/Domovoi

2. http://auntida.tripod.com/tomte.htmlhttp://auntida.tripod.com/tomte.html

3. Brothers Grimm. *The Elves and the Shoemaker*. Illustrated by Dominique Thibault. New York: Abbeville Press, 2001.

4. Bunce, John Thackra. *Fairy Tales, their Origin and Meaning*. Middlesex, UK: Echo Library, 2006.

5. Shepphard, Susan. http://www.zzzip.net/hpgh/cry_of_the_banshee.htm

6. Evans-Wentz, W.Y. *The Fairy Faith in Celtic Countries*. New York: Lemma Books, 1973. Evinity Publishing, Kindle version, 2009.

7. http://www.sacred-texts.com/neu/eng/efft/efft39.htm

8. Hartland, Edwin Sidney. *English Fairy and Folk Tales*. New York: Walter Scott Publishing, 2007.

# 4

MAGICK WITH TRADITIONAL
FAERIES, FAERY COURTS,
AND FAERY GODMOTHERS

Traditional sparkling faeries, miniature versions of humans but far more beautiful, ethereal, and with wings, are those most usually associated with faery magic. The sparkle detected around the bodies of faeries is like the halos around the heads of saints, a reflection of their spirit form that is made of the same white-gold shimmer around the outermost layer of the human aura where it joins the cosmos.

As they swiftly move, their shining aura appears to leave a trail of golden dust; this is also why the traditional faery godmother wand is seen as having light all around it.

## The Recording of Traditional Faery Lore

Through the ages, more has been recorded by myth collectors about traditional faeries and their faery courts than any other nature spirits. Celtic-rooted countries have become a major source of first-person accounts of opalescent shining faeries and a fertile ground for researchers, especially among the Victorians who were avid collectors and investigators in the field of the paranormal.

An unbroken faery tradition has continued from ancient Greece to present-day faery sightings. Greek philosopher Homer wrote in around 800 BCE in his *Iliad* an epic about the Trojan Wars, "Where 'round the bed where Achelous springs, the watery faeries dance in mazy rings." *Mazy* means "labyrinthine"; Achelous was a Grecian river rising in Epirus and emptying in the Ionian Sea.[1]

## Faery Courts

The faery court and courtier tradition are centred around a faery king and queen. These traditions existed from medieval times when it was associated with the Holy Grail quests, when the historical late fifth- and early sixth-century King Arthur became in literature a courtly king with many fey connections.[2] Indeed, Sir Lancelot was of faery blood.

Faery courts came to the forefront in the sixteenth century, partly because of the epic poem "The Faery Queen," written by the contemporary English poet Edmund Spenser in honour of Queen Elizabeth I who was identified with the faery Queen Gloriana.

William Shakespeare also described more beautiful human-sized faeries like Titania and Oberon and the malevolent Puck in his play *A Midsummer Night's Dream* that was first performed in 1590.[3] Oberon and Titania, the faery king and queen, were both noble and spiteful. Titania was the powerful downgraded Themis, the ancient Greek Titan Goddess of justice and order, and the mother of the Fates and the Seasons; Oberon was the fey, a somewhat cleaned up descendant of the pre-Christian Horned God of animals, the hunt, and winter.

But the most detailed information of the faery courts and specifically of the Irish faery race (the *Tuatha de Dannan*, who were also called the *Daoine Sidh*, the people of the Mother Goddess Danu) comes from the accounts of the nineteenth-century Irish folklorist and poet, Lady Jane Francesca Wilde (1821 to 1896), in her book *Ancient Legends, Mystic Charms, and Superstitions of Ireland* .[4]

She described the faery queen Oonagh who was the wife of Finvarra, King of the fey of the west of Ireland. "Her golden hair sweeps the ground, and she is robed in silver gossamer all glittering as if with diamonds, but they are dew-drops that sparkle over it. The queen is more beautiful than any woman of earth, yet Finvarra loves the mortal women best."

Finvarra, according to Lady Wilde, lured mortal women down to his faery palace by irresistible faery music where they remained as faeries. Though their friends and families mourned them, they led happy lives within the hill in a faery palace with silver columns and crystal walls. Of course, we have no way of knowing how many of these fey-kidnapped women were in reality abducted and killed, even by family members if they became pregnant outside wedlock or failed to produce children if married. Faeries remained a useful scapegoat. In the west of Ireland, it was said that young women were unable to resist the music of Finvarra and they might find themselves back in their beds in the morning but had been given the power of love potions and spells to seduce any man or to do ill.

## Faery Gifts

Faery gifts could be double-edged swords. While those who slept on faery hills were said to become skilled musicians, for others, the gift and memory of faery music was so beautiful yet beyond the abilities of mortals to reproduce, and could haunt a human musician to death. Turlough O'Carolan was one of the lucky ones. The famous blind Irish harpist bard from County Meath (1670 to 1738), was said to acquire his amazing melodies by sleeping out all night on the faery hillocks, according to another fey researcher, the Anglo-Irish poet and playwright William Butler Yeats (1865 to 1939), in his *Faery and Folk Tales of the Irish Peasantry.*[5]

The *Sidhe* were considered to envy humans. In spite of their fabulous gold and crystal palaces, they lacked immortality though they had power over nature and humans. They lived caught between mortality and immortality;

and possessing neither, they abducted young women at the height of fertility (when the young women were just married) to produce half-human children so they might attain a soul.

# Faery Music

## The Sounds of the Fey

Ralph Harvey, an English researcher and author of folklore whom I met at a festival, described to me how he was staying with friends in Enniscorthy, Ireland and he and his wife heard faery music. One afternoon, he and his wife Audrey stopped for a picnic in a glade by a stream. Immediately they heard the sound of a small but quite-clear orchestra. They decided to investigate, but realised the music was following them and would stop when they stopped and continue as they walked on.

The music continued to play until they stepped out of the glade. Though they searched, the area was deserted. That night at dinner, their hostess asked where they had been exploring and, when they told her, she asked if anything unusual had happened there. When Ralph mentioned the music, she said, "Oh, you were very lucky. You heard the faery musicians."[6]

# A Magical Ritual with Traditional Faeries

You have already learned several fey rituals. The following one is very powerful when you want a special or more formal ritual either for yourself or to carry out with others. It brings in a number of traditional faery kings and queens and their powers to act as guardians of the four elemental quarters of your magick circle. If you are working with other people, you can divide the ritual so you all play a part.

This format can be used for calling love, beauty, harmony, fertility, prosperity, and the increase of natural talents. Each of the fey kings and queens I name will offer particular strengths and gifts. You can choose four for each ritual, one for earth, air, fire, and water. Think of these as representing four blessings you can receive.

We will work only with the most positive aspects of the faery royalty, though of course their challenging powers can bring impetus for change.

## Bringing the Fey Kings and Queens into Your Life

- Copy the information below about the kings and queens into your fey journal. Add any other royal beings you encounter through the additional readings I suggest at the end of the book and in the source materials in each chapter. Have a page for each so you can add information from your own ongoing fey encounters in rituals, meditations, and dreams.

- Whenever you have a spare ten minutes, sit in your indoor faery place and light a white candle and play soft music that contains the sounds of nature within it.

- Each time, choose one guardian whose qualities you especially need and look into the candle flame. Do not force any visions, but picture a doorway of gold in the centre of the flame. Fire is a natural doorway into faery realms.

- When your eyes feel tired, close them and picture the candle flame within your mind. Allow it to expand until it fills your mind and see the golden doorway opening within it.

- The figures will be slightly smaller than humans with finer, often pointed features but very beautiful and shimmering.

- Be patient and your fey king or queen will appear, possibly accompanied by small faery attendants or elves.

- When the vision fades, allow the doorway to close and say, "Until we meet again, I give you my thanks for showing yourself to me and I ask your blessings."

- Leave the candle burning and scribble down your descriptions or draw or paint them in your journal. You will develop favourites and they may appear to you spontaneously in dreams and meditation and you will learn more and more about them.

## The Regal Fey Guardians and Their Powers

### Earth

*Suitable Offerings:* Flowers, herbs, tiny crystals, pure-white stones, petals (especially rose or dried lavender heads).

#### Geb

An elemental fey king whose throne is covered with silver and gold crystals. He is guardian of miners and others who work within the earth.

**Element:** earth

**Powers he can endow:** prosperity, skill in all practical crafts, renovations, moneymaking by slow but sure means, success in property matters, animals, older people, and finding and restoring what is lost.

#### Galadriel

Elven queen of the earth faeries, made famous in J. R. R. Tolkien's *Lord of the Rings*, a beautiful, wise shimmering faerie, with special powers of healing.

**Element:** earth and also sometimes air

**Powers she can endow:** Healing, uncovering talents, bringing out the best in self and others, love, fidelity, gifts in music and the arts, all that is long lasting, reconciliation.

#### Oonagh

Golden-haired Faery Queen of the west of Ireland. Wearing silver gossamer with sparkling, diamondlike dewdrops. Wife of Finvarra who, despite his wife's beauty, still seduces mortal women.

**Element:** earth and air.

**Powers she can endow:** Maintaining faith during difficult periods in a relationship, beauty and radiance, women's spiritual powers, reclaiming personal power and confidence when others try to take it away, wishes.

### Mab / Maeve

Warrior Queen of faeries and fey midwife. Seen variously as a tiny, motherly figure or in her alter ego as the powerful faery queen of the land, granting sovereignty, prosperity, and mastery over the changing life cycles of the woman as she can transform herself from old woman to battle mother to lovely maiden at will.

**Element:** earth and air

**Powers she can endow:** fertility, good pregnancy, safe childbirth, mothers, babies, and children, wishes, uncovering secrets, secret love, all small but significant matters, passion, transformation, and prosperity.

### Titania

Queen of the faeries and wife of Oberon with power over the harvests. According to Shakespeare, like Oberon, Titania had many lovers including mortals. In Greek mythology, she was daughter of Gaia, the Earth Goddess, and is linked with Diana, goddess of the moon and love.

**Element:** earth and air

**Powers she can endow:** beauty, radiance, romance, sexual magnetism, abundance, justice, restoring order out of chaos, love in middle and later life, and good luck.

## Air

*Suitable Offerings:* Feathers, granular incense, feathery grasses, seeds, ribbons.

### Paralda

A mysterious, misty being who lives on the highest mountain on earth, who shimmers in early-morning sunlight and breaks through the mist as occasional radiance.

**Element:** air

**Power she can endow:** the expression of hidden talents, higher spiritual powers, returning to life after sorrow or grief, recalling ancient wisdom and past worlds, and keeping a low profile in confrontational times or difficult situations.

### Puck

The trickster of the fey world, woodland green or black, boyish, fast moving, eloquent, brilliant at challenging the status quo and cutting through restrictions, ingenuity, inventiveness, happy travel, and image changing.

**Element:** air

**Powers he endows:** travel opportunities, overcoming obstacles with ingenuity, starting again, creating new opportunities and business, successful speculation, relocation, turning a challenge into an opportunity, surprises, and adventures.

## Fire

*Suitable offerings:* Tiny candles; a small, clear, crystal sphere; anything gold; a small mirror, golden fruit; and golden flowers.

### Aine and Grainne

Two Celtic sister faery sun queens who in pre-Christian times were solar goddesses. In very old legends, Grainne was the mother and Aine the daughter.

Aine was linked with fertility, healing, the flourishing of cattle and grain, and the cycles of the solar and lunar year, for she was also lady of the moon. In Christian times, Aine became the faery queen of Munster.

Greine or Grainne was the crone or wise woman sun goddess and was a patroness of herbalism. She awoke the fertility of the earth in the springtime. Her priestesses lived in round Griannon or sun houses. Like Aine she was downsized as the faery queen of Leinster, Ireland where her sacred hill *Cnoc Greine* is still a centre for folk and fey magic.

**Element:** fire and earth

**Power they can endow:** fertility, harmony with life cycles, herbal healing powers, bringing matters to satisfactory fruition, getting what is rightfully owed to you whether credit for work, recognition, promotion or money owed, inheritances and abundance, and prosperity.

## Oberon

King of the faeries and husband of Titania. He is sometimes considered the father of Puck by a mortal woman. Oberon and Titania his Queen represent the ultimate fey divine couple who control the abundance or otherwise of the land. Oberon is regal and powerful, a demigod, but can also be spiteful. However he uses Puck to do his nasty tricks rather than getting his own royal hands dirty.

**Element:** fire

**Powers he can endow:** authority, leadership, finding a powerful partner, knowledge, fulfilment of ambitions, lasting success and prosperity, and justice.

## Finvarra or Finbarr

King of the faeries of the west of Ireland. A shining being skilled at music and chess and with a fondness for human women, he also gave good harvests and strong horses to those he favoured. But he can use his music to make the unwary dance till they dropped.

**Element:** fire

**Powers he can endow:** musical abilities and all forms of performing arts, writing, poetry, and ability in speculation, learning new skills, competitions and competitiveness, and good luck.

## Djinn

A fiery elemental spirit who, being made of pure fire, is a glorious flamelike creature with flashing ruby eyes. He is never still and lives in the mystical Emerald Mountains, ruling all fire spirits.

**Element:** fire

**Powers he can endow:** inspiration, creativity, small miracles, granting wishes, travel, any swift-moving matters, change, and courage.

## Water

*Suitable offerings:* Anything made of silver or copper; dark and misty mirrors; a small container of milk which faeries love; sea shells; silver bells; oils or flower waters in a small bowl; water in which three pinches of salt have been added and swirled around with a small silver (not steel) knife.

### Necksa

Queen of the deep oceans who rides a chariot of pearl. Necksa is pulled by pure-white sea horses dressed in all the colours of the sea and has shells braiding her hair.

**Element:** water

**Powers she can endow:** good luck, travel, the answering of wishes, psychic powers, love, fertility, marriage, reconciliation, peace, peaceful endings, and new beginnings.

### Cloinda

Of the golden hair, Cloinda is the daughter of Manannan mac Lir who ruled over the sea and who had magical rainbow-healing birds. Cloinda took mortal lovers to faeryland, never to return. Once, however, she loved the young mortal Ciabhan so much she left the otherworld to live with him. But while Ciabhan was hunting, her father sent a faery minstrel to enchant her and carried her back in a magical sleep. She is seen on seashores either as a huge wave or a seabird seeking her lost love. So she is said to help parted mortal lovers reunite.

**Element:** water

**Powers she can endow:** reconciliation in love, calling lovers from overseas and from the past, wishes, healing, finding what is lost or has been taken away, lasting love and fidelity, psychic dreams, flowing with the cycles of life, and moving away with a partner from a familiar area.

*Manannan mac Lir*

Lord of the Otherworld Isles of the Blest as well as the Isle of Man and the Isle of Arran on which the magical cauldron of Annwn was kept. As a faery king, he caused mists to surround the Isle of Man, so keeping away enemies but also luring unwary boats on to the rocks.

Manannan was a guardian of the grail treasures and was a master magician. It was Manannan who decreed that the world of faeries and the world of humans should forever remain separate.

**Element:** water

**Powers he can endow:** protection, abundance, successful sea rituals, transformation, and happiness after partings and especially for shape-shifting and for youthfulness.

*Ran*

Golden-haired sea queen of the Norse world who was married to Aegir the sea god and it is said loved gold above all else. Her nine daughters were the waves and in both the Celtic and Norse worlds the ninth wave was believed to be the transition between the known and unknown worlds. She was very fierce and would drag sailors down to her watery palace.

**Element:** water

**Powers she can endow:** prosperity and the granting of wishes; protection of loved ones; reconciliation with those who are far away or who are estranged; and the return of missing people, pets, and items.

# A Traditional Wish-Granting Ritual

As this ritual has a number of stages, I will number them and you may like to practice the stages one at a time. If you do not want to carry out the whole ritual, just combine the stages that feel right.

## Stage 1: Preparing for the Ritual

- In advance, choose the combination of four faery kings and queens who offer the powers or wishes you most need. You may have all male or all female in some rituals. Your main purpose will be represented by the being you choose as predominant.

- If you prefer, picture your own stately fey being for each of the quadrants, giving each the characteristics of the relevant element in a traditional faery form and the qualities they can offer. These will come into your mind quite spontaneously. You can add these spontaneous fey beings to your list in your journal or fey diary. Allow a name for your fey noble beings to emerge. These personal faery kings and queens will grow in clarity the more you work with them.

- Now close your eyes and picture a shimmering circle of golden light, like the fey dust trailing from a faery wand.

- Visualise the faery of each quadrant. You are seeing them on the spiritual plane as if through a hole in a net curtain, but in time you may see them externally. The one whose gifts you most need will be brighter and more shimmering than the others.

- Collect in a small basket an offering for each of the fey guardians with the most for the guardian whose help you most seek.

- You may like to buy a crystal or wooden wand for your fey work or use a pointed crystal or a stick found near the place where you are working. Alternatively, make your own which is remarkably simple.[7]

## Stage 2: Casting a Faery Circle

- There are strong similarities to the circle you created around your outdoor nature-spirit place. If you wish, you can use your outdoor faery space, but still create this magical circle after stage 1.

• Outdoors, visualise a circle of light extending around you. It should be large enough to comfortably walk around and sit in the middle at least nine feet (two- and three-quarter metres) in all directions. It will be bigger if others are working with you.

• If you find it hard to visualize the size of the circle, set eight marker stones found nearby to form an outline.

• Stand in the centre of your circle and turn in all directions as you point your crystal or index finger outward directly ahead. In the Southern Hemisphere, turn sunwise which is counterclockwise; turn clockwise in the Northern Hemisphere. Turn until you have made a complete circle, still remaining in the centre. Picture light flowing from your crystal, wand, or finger and making a shimmering outline of light rising from the ground to about waist high so you are enclosed in a glowing circle.

• Now, physically walk around the outside of the circle of light three times, first clockwise in the Northern Hemisphere and counterclockwise in the Southern Hemisphere, then reverse the directions. For the third circuit, walk in the direction you began. This creates a triple circle of power and protection.

• As you cast this triple circle, say softly and rhythmically until you have completed all three circuits, "Lords and ladies of the fey, I encircle this place of sanctity, harmony, and tranquillity, and in beauty, joy, and humility I welcome now your presence."

• If you prefer, create a physical circle from leaves, dried herbs, or wildflower petals. If you are indoors, set plants or flowers in a circle to make connection with the fey. Again, walk around the outside of the circle.

• Repeat the words until you have cast your circle.

## Stage 3: Assigning the Elements

- Now you need to assign the quadrants of the circle according
  to their element unless you are in your regular outdoor space
  where you already have identified them.

- To do this, remove your shoes and walk once around the inside
  of the circle slowly, clockwise in the Northern Hemisphere and
  counterclockwise in the Southern Hemisphere. Allow the energies
  to flow upwards. Now go around the circle in the opposite direction
  even more slowly with your hands horizontal and pointing downward
  with your fingers slightly curved.

- Though you are in your outdoor place, you allowed the elements
  to come in any order. For formal fey magick, start by identifying the
  element associated with the guardian king or queen whose strengths
  you most need now.

- For example, if you need the healing of the shimmering elven queen
  Galadriel who is associated with the earth, walk around until you feel
  the steady pulse of the earth beneath your feet and you will discover
  that approximately a quarter of the circle vibrates in tune with the
  earth.

- Now you have identified your primary element, earth, choose your
  second elemental deity in order of priority and find their element
  by walking around the rest of the circle.

- For example, if you want the transformative, swift-moving energies of
  Puck (more of a prince than a king), the next quadrant you would seek
  is air where you will feel a light rippling sensation, like holding your
  hands over a fan, and again the impressions will last for approximately a
  quarter of the circle. There may not be precise divisions, as some places
  are more earth while others more fire, air, or water. You will always get
  the four elements within the circle formation that will combine in the

centre to form the fifth Akasha or Aether where the fey magick can be woven.

• Do the same for the third element.

• Fire will be felt as swift, warm, and very exciting but slightly unstable. Water will be flowing, cool, maybe quite turbulent like waves or a waterfall or perhaps smooth as a still lake or deep pool ruffled by a gentle breeze.

• If you use the same area again, you will know the elemental positions.

## Stage 4: Greeting the Fey Guardians

• Begin with the quadrant and guardian whose blessings you most need. Then, walking clockwise if you live in the Northern Hemisphere and counterclockwise in the Southern Hemisphere, pass from quadrant to quadrant, greeting the guardian of each element as you stand on the perimeter of the circle in the centre of the quadrant. Ask for a blessing related to their power. You may like to prepare and even write these in advance.

• Raise your arms shoulder-height and extend them on either side of your body with your palms flat facing upward as you greet each guardian. If this feels unnatural, just hold your arms in a way that feels right, maybe extended outward together, palms up about waist height.

• Face outward as you speak. You can use the fey names directly as long as you insert a positive adjective such as "good," "wise," or "gentle" in order to attract their best qualities.

• Say for example, "Paralda, wise mystical lady of the air, I welcome you respectfully to this faery circle and ask that you help me express my as yet unrevealed talent in . . . "

- If there really is no blessing you seek, change the greeting to "and ask that you help me in the way I most need your wisdom and gifts."

- When you have done this, walk, return to the centre, and face the direction of the guardian whose blessings you most seek.

## Stage 5: Making Offerings

- Now, make offerings to each beginning with the guardian whose blessings you most seek. Make an offering appropriate to each guardian; for example, a small container of milk for the water guardians. Walk either clockwise or counterclockwise according to your hemisphere. If doing the element weaving alone, raise your hands and thank the guardians. Turn around three times in each direction, clockwise first in the Northern Hemisphere and counterclockwise in the Southern Hemisphere and end by a final three circuits, nine in all, in the direction you began. Say, "May I walk always within the light of your blessings. The rite is ended."

## Stage 6: Closing the Ritual

- When you feel ready, walk in the reverse direction of your casting so you will end with the guardian with whom you began the ritual.

- Face each again and thank them, saying, "Wise Guardian of [name element and guardian's name], I thank you for your presence and your blessings. Until we meet again, I wish you peace and joy as you go to your world and I return to mine."

- You are not dismissing the faery kings and queens, for that would be disrespectful, but it is always important to mark the ending of a ritual and, like the end of any party or event, say goodbye and return to your own separate realms. Otherwise your energies will be buzzing.

- If outdoors, do something for the immediate environment. If indoors, water or tend your plants.

# Traditional Faery Sightings in the Modern World

Sparkling, winged faeries are much smaller than faery kings and queens, and belong to the court of the nobler faeries. They may also live together in troops, and these are the faeries most often seen by children. They are also natural guides and messengers to the magical otherworld and can lead you on mystical journeys during meditation or when you are sitting quietly in a beautiful place. You may have already met yours when you did the first meditation in chapter 1 from the faery who gave you your fey name.

Other faeries can appear at any time, often when totally unexpected, and may pop through a dimension door when you are relaxed and receptive. Karen is a businesswoman and healer in her forties living in an urbanised part of the Isle of Wight, a small island off the south coast of England. She described an experience she and her partner Sue shared where a traditional faery appeared to them as they were driving companionably in silence:

> *Sue and I were driving over Brading Down, enjoying the drive and not talking. I was changing from second to third gear when it seemed there was no speed; everything stopped, like being in another dimension or time warp. I saw out of the corner of my eye a shimmer, a twinkling light. Then, in front of my windscreen floated in so close I thought she would hit the windscreen, a tiny, perfect faery with golden ringlets, two- or three-inches high. She was like gossamer with a tiny pointed nose, shimmering wings, and tiny perfect legs. Her wings were translucent and rainbow-coloured like petrol on the road. She floated there for two or three minutes, but it seemed forever. She smiled at me as she floated down the windscreen. Then she was like a twinkling light again, gone out of sight. I asked Sue if she had seen anything and she said yes. I would not let her say more, but when we got home I made her write everything down and it was exactly the same description.*

## Urban Faeries

In the modern world, faeries are also frequently reported in urban backyards or homes. As town has replaced countryside in industrialised countries, so the faeries adapted to urban living. Some can be immensely comforting to a lonely child; accounts of adults who are still convinced they saw faeries as a child are particularly fascinating to me as a researcher of childhood psychic experiences.[8]

Libby, who lives in Liverpool in North West England, and now is in her forties, told me how she played with faeries when she was about five years old in her terraced home in the middle of the city. For one particular faery, Libby made a bed every night in her chest of drawers. Libby says the faeries were very tiny and very pretty and fun. Once at school in the playground some children would not let Libby join in their game. She felt very left out, so she lay down so her face was in the grass at the side of the playground. She could see her faeries in the blades of grass, but only, she said, if you put your face right down.

Urban faeries can be equally malevolent as rural ones, and they can take mischievous delight in bullying terrified children, taking on all kinds of shapes and forms to torment a sensitive child. Nicky, who lives on the Isle of Wight, England, and is now in her late thirties, told me, "As a child I quite frequently saw cartoonlike figures giving off their own light in my bedroom at night. They were not living creatures, but animated. There were sparks and then they appeared. They would fly away and come back. There were little men with big eyes pulling horrible faces."

Nicky was absolutely terrified and her mother, though she could not see the creatures, helped Nicky to drive them away, though they returned several times.

## Traditional Fey Folks Who Have Become National Institutions

The leprechaun has become a national emblem of Ireland and the leprechaun doll is one of the most popular souvenirs for tourists, said to transfer the good fortune of the actual spirit by a magical process.

The Irish leprechaun is a solitary creature. Leprechauns are described as small, old men dressed in green, sometimes with a leather apron, with buckled shoes and three-sided hats, a symbol of the ancient Irish triple god of whom the leprechaun is another downgrade.

Each leprechaun is said to possess a crock of gold. If a mortal, alerted by the sound of the leprechaun's hammer (the leprechaun is also a shoemaker), catches the leprechaun and holds him fast, he will promise to reveal the location of the gold.

However, the leprechaun is an expert trickster, and if the human takes his eye off him, even to blink, the leprechaun is gone. Should this fail, the leprechaun has two leather pouches. The first contains a magical silver coin that always returns to the purse no matter how many times it is given in payment. The second contains a gold coin which the leprechaun will give to the mortal to buy his freedom. But this coin will turn into leaves or ashes. So while the greedy human is admiring his newfound wealth, the leprechaun disappears and the crock remains undetected. However, they can be sociable with humans and will play the tin whistle.

## Faery Godmothers

The original faery godmothers were the Fate Goddesses, usually three sisters who were weavers or spinners of the web of destiny and controlled the fate not only of mortals but the deities. Once they were downgraded as faerie, they were separated into the *good* faery godmother, protectress and granter of wishes who endows the hero or heroine with a blueprint of future destiny, and the wicked faerie or witch. The earlier tradition and the faery legends merged quite naturally in many lands. For example, in Scandinavia where there was a huge overlap in the Norns, the Sisters of Fate who guarded the Well of Destiny or *Wyrd* ("fate"), and the later faery godmother stories of the Norn godmothers endowing infants with gifts at birth. For this reason, I have used the Norns as an example.

The Well of Urd or Wyrd was sited beneath one of the roots of *Yggdrasil*, the World Tree of Norse and Germanic myth. Yggdrasil, the World Tree, was fed by the Well of Urd in whose waters the three Norns, the Sisters of

Fate, gazed each morning to give guidance to the deities. This well contained cosmic knowledge from when the world began and the potential for the future of individuals and deities. The three sisters wove the web, both of the world and the fate of individual beings—mortals and gods. They visited each newborn infant to allot their blueprint, which they etched on wooden rune staves, magical symbols from the World Tree, and cast into the waters.[9]

The first Norn, Urdhr, the oldest of the sisters whose name means "fate" or "that which has become," always looked backward and talked of the past; in Viking tradition, the past influenced not only a person's own present and future but that of his or her descendants, both genetically and in the values transmitted from ancestors. The second Norn, Verdandi, whose name translates as "necessity" or "that which is becoming," was a young, vibrant woman. She looked straight ahead and talked of present deeds, which also influenced the future. Skuld, the third Norn, whose name is "being" or "that which will become," tore up the web as the other two created it. She was closely veiled and her head was turned in the opposite direction from Urdhr. She held a scroll which had not been unrolled; it told of what would pass, given the intricate connection of past and present interaction.

## The Transformation from Fate Goddess to Faery Godmother
In Norse legend that passed seamlessly into faery stories, the Norns once visited Denmark and went to the house of a nobleman whose wife had just given birth to their first child, a boy whom they named Nornagesta.

The first Norn promised that Nornagesta would grow to be brave and strong, the second that he would become rich and a great poet. But the third Norn was accidentally pushed out of the way by neighbours and angrily declared the child would live only until the taper at the bedside was burned through.

Seeing the mother's distress, the second Norn blew out the taper and gave it to the weeping woman, saying it should never be lit until her son wearied of life. The other predictions came true for Nornagesta. After his parents' deaths, Nornagesta kept the taper in the frame of his harp and for three hundred years fought bravely and sang great songs, never getting older. At last, he went to the court of King Olaf Tryggvesson who insisted the poet was baptised. As a sign of his new faith, Nornagesta lit the taper. When it burned through he died.

In Slavic folklore, Rodenica or Rozhenica was once the Lady and Creating Mother of the universe. When Christianity came, Rodenica was downsized to an ethereal white faery who, according to folklore, with her daughter visited newborn children to determine their future destiny.

## Faery Wells

The Norns predicted the future of gods and mortals in their magical well. A number of traditions of faery wells do date directly from these faery godmother or fate goddess connections, and the well faeries were consulted not only to give visions of future loves in dreams, but to bring the happy ever after (true faery-godmother style).

The most famous documented faery well is located at the top of a hill at Brayton Barf to the south of Selby in Yorkshire in the UK, but can no longer be accessed by the public. At some indeterminate date, the local abbot rededicated the well to the Virgin Mary but young women continued to visit it for insights into love.

One recorded case is that of a nineteenth-century servant girl in Yorkshire, England who visited this well, called the Faerie's Pin Well. It was so named after the custom of dropping silver pins in the water as offering to the particular faery godmother or wish granter who lived in the well.

The girl drank from the well, asking the faery of the well to bring her a dream of the man she would marry and that the event would thereafter be hastened. As tradition demanded, she fell asleep by the well whereupon her would-be lover dressed in wedding finery, brought her a wedding ring in her dream and the girl was taken to elf-land for feasting and revelry.

## Faery Godmother Well Magick

The following spell will identify a lover if one is around you or the identity of a yet-unknown one. As a bonus, the spell will telepathically call the lover into your life with the help of a faery godmother or two if the lover is slow coming; they might also help to increase commitment if it is right for you.

### You will need:

- A natural water source near which you can sleep or at least close your eyes for ten minutes. If you cannot find an ancient well or spring, find a lake or river on a camping ground and, like the lovers of old, sleep near the water in a tent or by renting a lakeside hut. You might even discover future love in the next tent or chalet.

- A silver-coloured coin, earring, charm, or a bent silver-coloured pin. If you can get a sterling-silver pin, that is best of all, but never iron. A broken brooch clasp can be adapted.

- A faery wand if you have one or a pointed stick found nearby.

### Timings:

- When spell casting at a well, carry out the ritual any afternoon; if you are staying near a lake, cast it at nightfall. Friday to Sunday are magical days that belong to the faery people—Friday afternoon or evening is best of all.

### The spell:

Cast your gift into the water to the spirit of the water (sometimes regarded as nine female spirits at sacred wells) saying six times:

> *"In my dreams come to me,*
> *My lover true that I may see.*
> *Lover true, do not tarry,*
> *Reveal the place where we shall marry."*

Close your eyes for ten minutes. If an evening ritual, go straight to sleep, whispering the words nine times, "Come, true love, come to me, over land and over sea, to where I wait in love for thee."

In your daydream or dream, you may recognise the place where the wedding takes place and maybe the identity of the bride or groom. If you do not dream, be patient as the dream may come on subsequent nights. You might also get clear signs about your future lover in the days ahead. All will be revealed over the coming months.

When you wake from your reverie, hold the wand or stick in your dominant hand, extending your arm straight ahead waist high and move it clockwise, continuously and smoothly, and move your other hand counterclockwise, arm extended at the same height and palm downwards, again rhythmically. Face the well and repeat nine times, "Come, true love, come to me, over land and over sea, to where I wait in love for thee."

Move your hand and the wand faster and faster and say the words faster until you can go no faster. Then, raise the wand and bring it straight down in a curve behind you and forward again on a final word: *Soon*. This will release the power into the cosmos.

In the next chapter, we will work with the spirits of the earth.

---

## Chapter 4 Sources

1. Pope, Alexander. *Homer's Iliad*. http://ebooks.adelaide.edu.au /h/homer/h8ip/book24.html

2. http://www.arthurian-legend.com/

3. Shakespeare, William. *A Midsummer Night's Dream*. http:// shakespeare.mit.edu/midsummer/full.html

4. Wilde, Jane Francesca. *Ancient Legends, Mystic Charms, and Superstitions of Ireland*. Barber Press, 2010.

5. Yeats, William Butler. *Fairy and Folk Tales of the Irish Peasantry*. Mineola, NY: Dover Publications, 2011.

6. Harvey, Ralph. *The Last Bastion*. Zambezi Publishing, 2004.

7. Eason, Cassandra. *Cassandra Eason's Complete Guide to Natural Magick.* Slough: Quantum/Foulsham, Kindle version, 2011.

8. Eason, Cassandra. *Psychic Power of Children.* Slough: Quantum/ Foulsham, 2005. (Libby, who lives in Liverpool in North West England and now is in her forties, told me how she played with faeries when she was about five years old, in her terraced home in the middle of the city.)

9. http://en.wikipedia.org/wiki/Norns

# 5

## NATURE SPIRITS OF THE AIR

S pirits of the air are most often with wings; they are light, ethereal, and generally less fixed to the earth than other nature spirits. Frequently, they live in
windy places such as hillsides, mountains, open plains, meadows, or grasslands.

Just as fire spirits are the most volatile of the nature essences, air spirits are
by their elemental nature the fastest moving in nature and form, changeable in
mood, and unpredictable. Air spirits are movers of energy, carrying seeds for
germination, stripping dead leaves from trees, and assisting birds on their migratory paths. They may frequently assume the form of birds or butterflies, for
example the Italian and Mexican *folletti* that shape-shift into butterflies to travel
on the wind, sometimes causing dust clouds (see page 113 in this chapter).[1]

A notable example of a noble air spirit is *sielulintu*, the golden Finnish
"soul-bird," on whose behalf small birds carry the souls of unborn children
to their new families and return souls on death to the heavens.[2]

You may come across nature essences who are nothing like the ones I
describe in this book, or varieties you read about elsewhere. Note down what
you see, sense or hear with times and dates in your special notebook or journal
and you may find that you become aware, for example, of sparkly air spirits
when there is imminent change in your life.

# The Power of the Air Spirits

Air spirits are empowered by the energy of the clouds, mountains, hills, and flowers in a meadow or on cold frosty mornings when the ice shimmers. A Celtic legend was told to me by an old lady many years ago when I was visiting the Isle of Skye in the days before the road bridge. It described fabulous rainbow butterflies that would settle like a cloud over fields of summer flowers and then disappear upward as if drawn by an air vortex. She said she had seen them as a child and that her grandma said the sky people were blessing the harvest.

## Attracting Air Spirits

Because air spirits, like all fey creatures, exist on the astral or spiritual plane, you can work with any kind regardless of where you live in the world. If you grow lavender, fennel, or any of the air fey plants listed below, you will attract benign air spirits. They will not stay long but stir the air wonderfully. They love any trees that are tall and whose tops sway in the wind, but you may get pelted with acorns or nuts as you walk through a plantation.

### Air-spirit Magical Associations

**Archetypal elemental spirit:** *Sylphs*, winged air spirits who live for hundreds of years and can, it is said, attain an immortal soul through good deeds. They reside on mountain tops. Sylphs may assume human form for short periods of time and vary in size from being as large as a human to being much smaller; they are usually seen in or as the effects of wind, for example a pile of leaves flying high in the air or sudden swirling mists.

**Air spirits ruler:** A mysterious misty being called Paralda who is said to dwell on the highest mountain on Earth.

**Favourite time of day:** dawn

**Favourite season:** spring

**Energy:** active

**Air-spirit characteristic:** initiator and inventor

**Elemental tool:** blade

**Air spirit ritual substance:** incense or smudge

**Favourite colours:** yellow, purple, and pearly grey

**Psychic gifts they offer:** clairaudience

**Polarity:** God

**Air-spirit energy-raiser:** music, song, and chanting

**Deities:** maiden, spring, and flower goddesses; gods of light; sky father gods; messenger and healing deities; and star deities (also sometimes ruled by fire)

**Archangel:** Raphael, the traveler and healing archangel and ruler of the four winds carries a golden vial of medicine with a traveler's staff; he is dressed in the colours of early morning sunlight, a green healing ray emanating from his halo.

**Air-spirit crystals:** amethyst, angelite, blue opal or angel aura, blue lace agate, clear crystal quartz, citrine, danburite, diamond, sapphire, lapis lazuli, sodalite, sugilite, and turquoise

**Air-spirit animals and birds:** bees, butterflies, birds of prey, moths, white doves, flocks of silvery or blue birds, and swallows

**Air-spirit fragrances:** acacia, almond, anise, benzoin, bergamot, dill, fennel, lavender, lemongrass, lemon verbena, lily-of-the-valley, marjoram, meadowsweet, papyrus flower, peppermint, and sage

**Ailments and body parts especially healed by air spirits:** illnesses and injuries related to the breasts, chest, lungs, throat, brain, immune system, metabolism, thyroid, adrenal and pituitary glands; anxiety, depression, and other illnesses

**Sense:** speech, smell, and hearing

**Positive qualities and strengths offered by air spirits:** clear focus, impetus for positive change, ability to communicate clearly, concentration, versatility, spontaneity, positivity in new beginnings and expanding horizons, persuasiveness, intelligence, fair-mindedness, logic, independence, clarity, good memory, mental dexterity, optimism, teaching abilities, poetic and musical gifts, commercial and technological acumen, healing gifts through orthodox medicine or from higher spiritual sources

**Less desirable qualities:** sarcasm, spite, gossip, fickleness, superficiality, emotional coldness, dishonesty, pedantry, unwise speculation or gambling.

**Air-spirit places:** mountaintops, hills, towers, the sky, pyramids, open plains, tall buildings, balconies, roof gardens, clouds, wind

**Materials for attracting air spirits:** feathers, feathery grasses, ceiling mobiles, long, trailing scarves, wind chimes, fragrances, clouds, mist, and bird-call music

**Astrological signs:** Aquarius, Gemini, Libra

**Planets:** Mercury, Jupiter, and Uranus

**Empowerment to call the power of the air spirits:** "Fly free and carry me to places of beauty that I may soar and rise through the skies."

**Use air-spirit magick for:** new beginnings, safe and happy travel, house moves, learning, passing tests and examinations, career, interviewing, money making through initiative, speeding up slow-moving matters, justice through the legal system, inventions, medicine or conventional healing and surgery, self-employment, wishing well for young people, successful buying and selling, protection against road or travel accidents, learning languages, success in writing, and jobs in the media.

# Discovering Spirits of the Air

## Sylphs

Sylphs are described in the ancient Greek and Roman tradition but are found in many lands as winged air spirits or sprites.[3] The Classical sylphs are very slender and graceful, like transparent ballerinas, constantly moving as they float just above the ground or fly through the sky, creating wispy trails of light or mist. Some say they were seen by early people who thought they were deities; later, they were thought to be angels. They differ from angels in that they are much mistier and transparent and do not focus on human concerns or act as guardians.

It has been speculated that the Butterfly Goddess of Minoan Crete, whose images date from about 4000 BCE, was in fact an evolved nature being of the air. The fabulous winged butterfly is a form sylphs frequently adopt. Of course this is just one theory.

They are sometimes depicted with huge wings, their bodies the size of a human body but far more ethereal and slender. Once believed to control the weather and direct the winds, they have also been described from classical times onward as taking the form of huge, white graceful birds, like gigantic swallows. Sylphs sometimes appear in bird or butterfly form or as streaks in the sky just before a storm, leaving grey trails behind them.

You will find sylphs in wide-open spaces, wilderness areas, and meadows as well as higher ground. They protect their own areas of land or a particular mountain or hill and may sometimes cause mists that shroud a place even if the area all around is clear. Sylphs do not communicate directly with humans, though those who have seen them, usually very fleetingly, talk about being touched by a breeze that stirs the soul with happiness and brings a sense of freedom to try new avenues.

They carry new seeds for germination and oversee cross-pollination of species as well as ensuring that the insect world continues to flourish and remain in balance. If a place is under threat, sylph activity and sightings will increase. One example is a mountain on the island of Lewis in the Outer Hebrides off the West Coast of Scotland known as *Na Mointeach*, "the Old Woman of the Moors"; it is also known as "Sleeping Beauty," "Sleeping Mother," or "Sleeping Goddess." The mountain is so called because it appears like a sleeping goddess when it is seen from the local Callanish stone circle. Every 18.6 years, the moon appears to be born from the Goddess figure when the moon emerges from between her legs. A proposed wind farm would destroy the sacred site.

## Jenny's Sylph Encounter

Jenny comes from the South of England every year to Lewis, an island that is full of sacred places. She told me,

> *I had visited the mountain many times and loved watching from the centre of the Callanish Circle the goddess resting on the mountain.*
>
> *I had heard about the problems with the proposed wind farm and so was specially determined to visit the unspoiled spot once more in case the appeals against the destruction did not succeed.*
>
> *It was a clear, blue day. Suddenly the mountain was surrounded by what I can only describe as spirals of mist that seemed to whirl in the air like flocks of birds, except they were transparent. The mist spirals rose and seemed to dance around the mountain top. Then they were gone. The area was deserted, but someone else must have seen them. Or was it just me? I looked in the local paper and there was nothing unusual reported.*

## Sylph Encounters

Like much air-spirit magick, sylph magick is less structured than that of other elemental spirits, though they respond well to bubbles, kites, prayer flags, and feathers (see page 125 in this chapter for these forms of air-spirit magick). Use only natural fabrics.

Sylphs will make you lighthearted, spontaneous, and joyous if you flow with their energies. As a result, your mindset will be looser, much more open to new ideas, and welcoming to change. After a sylph encounter, anything seems more possible. This might be making plans to see a place to which you long to travel or doing something amazingly out of character (at least the character others impose on you) that brings you sudden, spontaneous happiness in a previously dull world.

- Go somewhere open, such as a grassland, hill, or mountain. Summer is sylph time, but you can find them on any day when there is a breeze or as mist is lifting—or even over a shimmering snow field.

- Wear loose clothes. Tie long, thin scarves in a delicate fluttery material such as silk around each of your wrists and another around your neck. Hold one from each hand.

- Stand so the breeze is behind you and trail the scarves behind you in so you move with the wind.

- Look ahead and you will either see externally or sense shimmering trails of sunlight or mist even on a clear day and maybe ethereal shapes swooping and soaring like swallows. Close your eyes and you will see them clearly in your mind's vision.

- Even if you sense nothing at first, move with spiralling steps as the breeze gently pushes and tugs at the fabric; let the sylphs, like graceful, transparent, slender dancers with trailing robes, appear in your mind. Before long, you will connect with this most ethereal, bubbling, floating energy.

- When you are tired, sit in an open space and let the world go by. When you rejoin the world, retrace your path, spiralling back to everyday life. You will realise the wind is not against you even though you are walking into it, but that you can flow into the slipstream.

- Whenever you are stressed, close your eyes. If necessary, put on the air conditioning or a fan (warm air on a cold day) and move in your mind with your sylphs.

# Sylphs as Birds

Swooping birds that are blue, white, grey, or silver, especially flocks of swallows or doves, are also special sylph birds. If you find it hard to connect with sylph power or any other air-spirit energy because you are very logical, try the following exercise to relax your mind into seeing what logic finds it hard to accept. Migratory times in your region are especially good. In Central France where I often stay, the autumn sky is filled with calling black cranes migrating back from Africa through Spain and returning south in the summer.

- Sit or lie where there is an open horizon and a flying flock of birds overhead. Half-close your eyes and absorb the sounds and fragrances of the scene. Look not at the birds, but the shapes they are making as they fly.

- Allow your eyes to go into soft focus by looking slightly to the side and beyond the swirling mass, so that the birds are on the outer ranges of your vision.

- Now, allow some of the birds to naturally take on their sylph form, for sylphs often fly with birds as well as in bird form. *Feel* the crisp air and the sensation of flying free.

- Grey and white wispy clouds close to the birds may also take on sylph forms.

- Each bird and sylph will exude light, so follow the natural outline of one prominent bird that you may perceive initially as pale grey or blue; then add other outlines to the field of vision. Gradually, the sylph energies will change to swirling, shimmering silver luminescence, individual rainbow spirals within the growing, swirling light mass.

- The aura around the flock of birds as well as the individual energies will also change as the sylph energies become more prevalent and merge with the other bird auras, like gentle waves tinged by a silvery moon. You may perceive silver, pale-grey, or white flashes around the whole moving flock.

• Continue looking until it becomes an effort and you want to close your eyes, in which case let the sky aura naturally fade and rest.

• When you feel refreshed, stand up, turning around and around in both directions until you are dizzy and feel as if you are floating. For a second or two, you may experience the sensation of being no longer earthbound. Sylph connection will flood through you, bringing energy and excitement even for daily life.

• Scribble images of your personal sylphs. If you look on the Internet, you may find similar pictures reproduced from old books.

## Other Sylphlike Beings

In Italy and Mexico, the *folletti* (plural also for male and female) and the male counterparts, the *folletto,* resemble mischievous six-year-old children when earthbound. They are very slight with backward-pointing feet and are almost transparent. Males and females alike travel on the wind, creating mini dust storms or sudden uprushes of petals even when the air is still, as they fly suddenly upward in their flock, the usual mode of travel.[4] Depending on whether they are in a good mood or not determines whether they shower passing mortals in petals or dust for fun. There are different varieties of folletti, for example the *Abruzzo Mazamarelle*, a folleto about two feet high, wearing a flower or covered with flowers, or in the form of a grasshopper.

Folletti are also perceived as butterflies, though most are generally benign. Like all earth spirits, they are ambivalent to humans and some can be vicious. More aggressive folletti travel in whirlwinds, called wind knots, and create storms that destroy crops and property and bring floods just for the sake of it. Others are like the incubus and succubus, sexual predator spirits, for example the *Machinge*, a Sicilian folletto who violates women. Malevolent folletti are also said to try to induce madness. It may be as with other apparently vicious nature spirits, they were blamed for human crimes or natural disasters, in more superstitious times. Saints were invoked to protect against the nastier aspects of folletti and brown-haired women seem able to banish them also.

## Air Spirits as Butterflies

Folletti butterflies are tinier and more transparent than sylph ones, but both kinds will be brilliantly coloured.

I have already mentioned the Butterfly Goddess who appeared as a Crowned Butterfly around 4000 BCE in Minoan Crete, a centre of goddess and bull worship. But an equally important traditional Butterfly Goddess who also is a form of higher air spirit is Hina from the Polynesian tradition of the Pacific Islands. Hina is called the Creatrix of the world, Lady of the Moon, and her spirit is said to be contained in every woman, for she was the first woman. These deity associations make sylphs and folletti and any other air spirit who takes butterfly form an important icon for women, especially for any regeneration, new opportunities, and new beginnings.

- In summer, sit near flowers that attract butterflies such as lavender and look through half-closed eyes as different ones settle. A number of towns have butterfly farms or indoor gardens where even in the winter you can dance in your mind with your butterfly sylphs or folletti.

- Devise a chant for your magical air-spirit butterflies, for example, "Butterfly spirit with rainbow wings, who dances today with no regrets of yesterday or fears of tomorrow, open my heart to joy and new beginnings."

- Whisper the words or say them in your mind over and over again mesmerically as you focus on one particular air-spirit butterfly. You will easily be able to identify this air-spirit butterfly by the power it exudes, its brilliant colours, and your sense that it is watching you. Feel the fluttering of joy and hope you may not have felt for a long time.

- Slow the chant and, when your butterfly flies away, close your eyes and let the magical creature take its full spirit form in your mind's vision and fill you with the impetus to reach out for what or whom you want most.

- Take your time afterward and sit or walk among the flowers.

## The Light Elves

In Norse cosmology, light elves are the higher forms of elves, characterized by their light blond or golden hair and are the true air-spirit elves. Gandalf, immortalized by Tolkien as the master wizard, was an elven king. From Tolkien we also learn of Galadriel, the lovely elven queen who rules over all earth spirits, but is herself a being of the air. Elves also appear throughout the folklore of northern and western Europe.

In Scandinavia, light elves—like their darker brothers, the earth spirits, whom I write about in chapter 6—are the same size as humans but slender and perfectly formed with delicate, pointed features. They alone among the fey people seem to have maintained a form of immortality and freedom from aging.

The Viking fertility god Freyr, considered one of the race of Vanir or nature gods or higher air spirits, was Lord of the Elves and of Alfheim, the home of the light elves at the top of the Norse World Tree, close to the realms of the deities. Freyr had two elven attendants called Byggvir and Beyla. [5]

In pre-Christian times in Scandinavia, at the beginning of winter around the autumn equinox, the woman of the house would initiate a ceremony dedicated to the elves and ancestors to bring fertility and prosperity through the winter. No strangers were admitted and few details are known of this ancient practice.

Marriages between elves and mortals were much prized in the Scandinavian world. For example, the Viking hero Hagni had a human mother who was a queen and his father was the elf Aldrian. As a result the hero inherited the qualities of nobility, courage, and leadership through the maternal line; from his father he acquired the skill of magic, archery, and the ability to understand all the creatures of the earth and even speak to the trees. In addition, elven armour and a helmet rendered him invincible and invisible when necessary. In later times, the light elves became known for being beautiful female elves with an elven king to care for them.

## Elven Beings

In northern and western Europe, elves tend to be smaller. Like the Scandinavian elves, they are always beautiful young men and women, invariably with wings, and live in forest glades and flower meadows. They are creatures of the sun and of moonlight and are famed for wondrous pipe and fiddle music, singing and dancing, and skill with a bow.

Prehistoric flint arrowheads were called "elf shot." In folklore through to the 1900s, these were thought to be faery arrows used to enchant humans. This may be a memory carried in myth that the Neolithic tribes were very small and may have hidden in the forest and fired arrows at the tall invaders. The elf shot was attributed with many healing properties as well as the power to grant invisibility to the wearer and the ability to see elves.

Circles of small edible mushrooms rather than inedible toadstools like lesser elves and faeries indicate places where these elves dance at full moonlight. At dawn on the morning after a full moon, a mortal might run clockwise around the circle nine times, cast a pure white pebble into the middle, and make a wish aloud; it is said that the wish would be granted by the next full moon.

The elves could turn nasty if offended and could destroy cattle, spoil hunting or even, in old legends, spirit away humans who came upon their revels and accepted elven food. Were any human to come across the elves dancing and join in (or even pause to watch), he or she would dance for what seemed like a whole night; but when morning came many years would have passed. A special tune called "The Elf King Song" was said to be the most wonderful tune in the world, but if mortal musicians played it they would have to play until they dropped, unless someone cut the fiddle strings.

Danish elves would take newly risen dough and food from larders and stores. Unlike faeries that borrow from humans but repay, generally, the elves would not leave gifts or favours in return for what they took. The elves in Denmark were described as being only two dimensional, being hollow when seen from behind. Scandinavian *Huldre* folk were also described sometimes with a similar hollow appearance, an illusion since fey people are not made of material substance anyway.[6]

Elven energies are inspirational and excellent for all creative ventures, whether music, dancing, singing, art, or writing—and also for any sporting activities. Even if you do not consider yourself talented, you may find reviving an old interest opens up a new source of income or leads to new friendships as a result of elven inspiration.

- Go into the forests or fields and look for a faery circle of mushrooms or toadstools (do not touch them as some can be poisonous if you get them on your fingers).

- The morning after the full moon is best, but you can do it any morning, especially if there is plentiful dew on the grass. If there are no natural fey circles, make one using white stones, creating a circle of light in your mind, or walking around in a circle to mark the place psychically as you did in your formal faery ritual described in the previous chapter.

- Walk around the outside of the circle nine times clockwise, regardless of the hemisphere you live in, holding an air crystal such as purple amethyst, blue turquoise, clear quartz, or a perfectly round, white stone in your dominant hand.

- When you have completed the ninth circuit, hold the stone or crystal up to your lips in cupped hands. Blow on it slowly and softly three times as though blowing petals to the wind, saying a word between each breath, "Whatever—my—gift ... "

- Blow three times more, and saying one word again between the breaths, "hidden—lost—forgotten ... "

- Blow three final times, saying one word again between breaths, "elves—restore—release."

- Cast the crystal into the centre of the circle. You may have a flash in your mind of yourself within the elven ring singing, dancing, painting, reading your published work, practising healing, turning cartwheels, or being a ski champion—surrounded by beautiful light elves.

- Do not enter the elf circle, not because you will be spirited away (at least I am fairly sure you would not be) but because it is a private fey space.

- Leave a few small cakes or tiny oat biscuits near the edge of the circle.

- Spend time in the forest or outdoors for a while. Within a week or two, you will have seen an opening for your talents or have rediscovered your old guitar or art materials in a cupboard.

## Air Sprites

Some air spirits are hard to define or categorise and are called *sprites*. Air sprites flash in and out of vision like dancing sunbeams and are almost always greyish to silvery white with iridescent shimmers like bubbles. This is why bubble magick is so effective.

## Air–Nature Bubble Spell

You can send wishes into the air in the form of bubbles. These rise high and can carry them to the air sprites who will transform your dreams and desires into actuality. You can choose any wish, not only in those areas traditionally ruled by air. Wednesday and Thursday are especially good days for air-sprite wish magick.

### You will need:

- A bubble blower and bubbles. You can use a child's bubble-blowing set or make environmentally friendly bubbles with a pure liquid soap and distilled water.

- You can make a bubble blower out of any circle such as twisted wire or even the end of a straw dipped into the bubble mix.

- For a giant bubble wand for big wishes, twirl a coat hanger into a perfect circle, bending the hook to make a handle and taping it so it is not too sharp to hold.

- Making your own solution enables you to more easily empower it.

### Time and place:

Bubbles blow best on a cloudy day or after rain when it is not too cold.

### The spell:

- Make your bubble solution. Use three parts of an environmentally friendly liquid soap, washing up liquid or baby shampoo; seven to ten parts of distilled water (some people recommend very warm water but I use cold); and one part of glycerine. Glycerine is not essential but gives lovely rainbow bubbles. You can make more or less of this mixture, according to the size of your bubble blower and the number of bubbles you want to blow. It is a good idea to make plenty as you can repeat the spell weekly for a month for a longer-term wish and it can be stored in lidded containers.

- Put the ingredients into a bowl, mix gently with a whisk or spoon, saying softly over and over again: "You spirits of the air: sprites, sylphs, and rainbow butterfly folletti, aid my wish that it may travel to the skies and be transformed."

- When the mixture is bubbly, shake it ten times, naming your wish ten times.

- Put the bubbles in a sealed container. As late on Wednesday or Thursday afternoon as possible, go to a hilly place or open a window upstairs.

- Open the bubble mix and blow; recite the mixing chant three times and naming your wish three times. If you are using a commercial bubble, this will empower the mix.

- Blow the first bubble; as it floats away, say, "Wish fly free, from my thoughts to actuality."

- Continue blowing and wishing (more than one wish if you like), for each wish repeating the wish chant as you release each bubble, until you feel you have blown enough bubbles. Thank the sprites of the air and scatter seeds in thanks.

- If you want to really connect with the spell, beforehand practice blowing bubbles with your hands. Put the bubble mix in an open flat container, dip your hands in it, lock your thumbs, and slowly make a circle with your joined hands. Gently blow. This was taught to me by a friend's child and is totally magical once you master it.

- Repeat the spell weekly for four weeks or longer if you wish, if possible on a Wednesday or Thursday afternoon in the same location.

## Dandelion Clock Travel or Expansion Spell

When we release spores from dandelions, we are launching young faery forms into the air and they will carry our wishes into the ether where they can be transformed into reality. Dandelion spores spells or any other thistle-borne air-sprite spells are particularly good for travel and relocation as well as for launching new businesses or creative ventures.

## Timing
Whenever you find a dandelion clock or another thistle with spores.

## The spell:
When you find a dandelion, name your dream and say, "You sprites of air as you fly free, make this dream true by [name your time frame]."

Blow the dandelion clock as hard as you can, and keep on blowing until all the spores are gone.

# Air-Sprite Spell
# for Travel Plan or Journey

## You will need:
Four dandelion clocks, a small neck or waist pouch to carry them in, and a directional compass (optional).

## Timing
On a Wednesday morning.

## The spell:
- Carefully put your dandelion clocks in the pouch so the spores do not come off in transit and climb to the top of a hill.

- By estimating or using a compass, find the direction of your chosen or desired destination. Face it and say, "North, south, east, west, take me where I love the best, to [name the place you want to be], you spirits of the air."

- Hold the purse between your hands to empower it with your hand energy centres.

- Spin around nine times holding the purse, clockwise in the Northern Hemisphere and counterclockwise in the Southern Hemisphere. As you spin, say, "Far from home, May I roam, Far to fly, O'er sea or sky,

Take me where I love the best, to [name the place you want to be], you spirits of the air."

- Take the dandelion clocks out of the purse one by one. Starting with your chosen direction, blow one for each of the main four compass directions; as you do, say, "Fly far, fly free, 'cross land and sea. With you I go. Let it be so, you spirits of the air."

- Run or walk fast down the hill; as you go, recite your chosen destination as a mantra.

- When you get home, make a step, however small, toward planning your trip or making preparations for your journey.

## The Spirits of the Winds

Wind spirits, former deities, feature in myths from ancient Greece to native North America. In Iroquois myth, Gaob, the Lord of the Winds, appointed animal guardians for each of the four winds so that the winds' power would not overwhelm the world. He called the bear and tied him with a leash to control the herds of the north winter winds. The moose became protector of the herds of the eastern stormy skies. The panther was tethered to be guardian of the rainy west winds. The gentle fawn led the herds of the warm south winds out to graze on sunny days.

The four winds were given names and personalities in Greek and Roman myth where they were four brothers, sons of Eos or Aurora (the Goddess of the Dawn). Aeolus or Aiolos was keeper and father of the winds and lived on the floating island of Aiolia. He released the winds on instructions of the deities. The north wind ruler is called Boreas; he has brown wings, a dragon's tail, a rain cloud cloak and streaming white hair, and he was very tempestuous. The east wind's ruler is called Apheliotes, the youngest of the brothers and is always impatient to be away, flying through the sky scattering clouds. The ruler of the south wind is called Notus, most amiable of the winds, filled with sunlight and he emits sparkling light beams in his wake.

Finally, Zephyrus rules the west wind. He is a gentle wind, married to Iris, goddess spirit of the rainbow, and fills the sails of boats with breezes when they become becalmed.

## Making an Air-Fey Wish and Prayer Tree

Prayer sticks or trees consist of feathers or written messages attached to a stick or a branch fixed in the ground in an open space. They release petitions, entreaties, or blessings as the feathers or paper blow away in the wind. Prayer trees are found in cultures from Tibet to native North America; in more recent years, they have become a focus for collective peace rituals as well as private use worldwide. If you do want to use prayer sticks or trees in a more authentic manner, there are a number of excellent Native American websites belonging to specific nations you can contact.[7]

We will use this practice to work with the four main wind spirits to release wishes, blessings, or requests to the cosmos. They are especially effective for long-term projects or plans that usually take longer to come to fruition.

Each wind spirit is accompanied by numerous wind sprites, not identified by name.

## Wind-Spirit Magick Using a Prayer Tree

- Each wind has its own power.

- The north wind brings about endings, blowing away what is no longer needed in your life and banishing negative influences, fears, or bad habits. His empowerment, which you can recite as you tie the north-wind feather to your tree in your own rituals, is, "I cast away what I no longer need with blessings."

- Use the east wind for new beginnings, new perspectives, changes in direction in your life, travel, self-employment, relocation, and for blowing away inertia or stagnation. His empowerment is, "I change as I seek ever-expanding new horizons."

- Work with the south wind for bringing all manner of good things into your life, especially good luck and good news, growth and expansion of any venture or opportunity, success in speculation, loans and money negotiations, and for filling yourself with power and confidence. His empowerment is, "I embrace joy, life and good fortune."

- The west-wind spirit will bring fertility, blessings, healing, peace, and the impetus to bring existing ventures to fulfilment. His message is, "I offer reconciliation and accept what cannot now be changed."

- Inviting wind from all four directions into any spell, as opposed to just one wind, is really going to get the spell's effect moving. If you are at an impasse or need some urgent action or radical change, call Boreas from the north, Apheliotes in the east, Notus in the south, and Zephyrus in the west. If you wish, ask their power animals to stand by them: the bear, the moose, the fawn, and the panther.

## Making Your Air-Spirit Prayer Tree

Air-spirit prayer trees traditionally vary in size from a large, forked staff that is shoulder height; a tall, uprooted branch with several smaller branches; or an actual growing tree. There is no reason a living leafy tree cannot be a prayer tree.

For magick of the four wind spirits, you will need four distinctive branch offshoots on your prayer tree so that you can have these smaller branches in approximately the four directions for the four winds on which to hang the wind feathers or messages.

Use a compass to find your directions. You can of course change the wind guardian based on the hemisphere and qualities of the winds; for example, if the wind blowing from the south is colder, as in places in the Southern Hemisphere like Australia, Notus then takes on the qualities of the fierce, banishing north winds. If you have an ocean immediately to the east as in eastern Australia, you could make your eastern air spirit the watery one. If easier, use my directions as all magick is on the astral plane and the physical matters less; it is most important to be consistent.

Before you begin, strip off the foliage from a large, dead branch or use one that has been lying a while and is quite dry.

- If you are setting a branch permanently to act as a prayer tree, dig a deep hole and fill the base with stones to secure the tree in all weathers.

- You can also erect a temporary one whether for private or collective use. On top of a small mound is ideal or any open area where the breezes will catch and energise the feathers or written messages, but not so exposed that they will instantly rip off.

- Alternatively, you can use a tree in a garden, local park, or forest.

## Preparing the Four-Winds Air-Spirit Spell

- Collect feathers from different birds; either find ones on the ground or go to a bird conservancy where you can buy more exotic kinds. (I have written in detail about feather magick, the magical significance of different birds, as well as air magick in my *Complete Guide to Natural Magick*,[8] should you wish to learn more about the topic.) Here you are using each feather as a means of connecting magically with air; it does not matter if you do not know its individual magical significance. Use light-coloured feathers for wishes or to attract what you need; use dark-coloured feathers for banishing what you no longer want or that which is destructive.

- Decide on the purpose or purposes of the spell and name the feathers according to the corresponding wind guardian. For example, if you wanted to banish misfortune you would name the feather for Boreas, the spirit of the north wind.

- If you prefer, write the message on a strip of paper. If you wish, you can have a feather and message for each direction, but this is not essential.

- When you have named the required number of feathers (a maximum of one for each direction) or have written your messages, take them to your prayer tree with strong thread to attach them (for messages you can punch a hole on the end of the strip of paper).

- Hold each feather or paper close to your lips in turn and whisper three times what or whom you wish to call into your life or to blow away what is redundant. Then tie it to the tree.

- Smudge around the tree with a lighted sagebrush, cedar smudge stick, or sage or pine incense and ask the air sprites to move near. Begin with the north even if you did not tie a feather there; stop at each of the four cardinal directions and make a spiral of smoke in the air.

- In the north say, "I call Boreas, the wise spirit of the north, to carry this, my prayer."

- In the east say, "I call Apheliotes, the wise spirit of the east to carry this, my prayer."

- In the south say, "I call Notus the wise spirit of the south to carry this, my prayer."

- Finally, in the west say, "I call Zephyrus the wise spirit of the west to carry this, my prayer."

- Then return to the north and raise the smudge stick to the sky, saying "I call the wise spirits of the sky to carry this, my prayer."

- Finally point the smudge towards the earth at a forty-five-degree angle and say, "I call the wise spirits of the earth to carry this, my prayer."

- Then, make seven smoke spirals over your head for the six directions, north, east, south, west, the sky, the earth while saying, "May all be fulfilled when right it is to be."

- Leave the feathers or messages to be blown away or decay as nature chooses.

## Calling on the Wind Spirits for Faster Changes

- For a faster-moving matter where you do not want to wait for the feathers to blow away, visit an open place on a windy day. Face the four directions starting with north, calling the four brothers by name, starting with Boreas and ending with Zephyrus. Though you have four wishes, there will be one that is most important. After saying the words below associated with your wind, add, "This is what I do most urgently desire."

- Face north and ask Boreas to blow away anything that is restricting you—a seemingly immoveable situation, destructive person, or unwelcome ties to the past. Name what you are losing and thank the spirit of the north wind.

- Face east and call Apheliotes. Ask him to bring the new beginning you need—desired travel or new opportunities. Name the change you seek and thank the guardian of the east wind.

- Face south and call Notus. Ask him to bring good fortune, prosperity, health, or success. Name what you seek and thank the spirit of the south wind.

- Face west and call Zephyrus. Ask him to bring fertility, healing, peace, justice, and reconciliation. Name what you seek and thank the spirit of the west wind.

- Turn around clockwise nine times, reciting the wind-spirit names, then counterclockwise nine times, and finally clockwise nine times ending as you face north again.

- Now say, "May the spirits of the winds carry my wishes to actuality." Name your most urgent wish and repeat, "This is what I most urgently desire and I thank you wise sprites for your presence and your swiftness. Until we meet again."

- The induced dizziness often gives a momentary out-of-body flying sensation in which you become a wind sprite. Sit or lie down, steady yourself, and enjoy the experience.

In the next chapter we will encounter the spirits of the earth.

---

## Chapter 5 Sources

1. Folletti, http://www.oocities.org/pookaplace/misc/home /folletti.htm

2. Snunit, Michal. *The Soul Bird*. New York: Hyperion, 1999.

3. http://www.crystalinks.com/sylphs.html

4. Lindow, John. *Norse Mythology: A Guide to Gods, Heroes, Rituals, and Beliefs*. Oxford University Press, 2002.

5. Mack, Carol K., and D. Mack. *A Field Guide to Demons, Vampires, Fallen Angels, and Other Subversive Spirits*. New York: Arcade Publishing, 2011.

6. www.shamanicvisions.com/sacredplaces_folder/prayertree .html. Comprehensive and well-illustrated site on prayer trees and sticks.

7. Eason, Cassandra. *Complete Guide to Natural Magick.* Slough: Quantum/Foulsham, Kindle, 2011.

8. www.geocities.com/felicitax/magic.htm. The Feathers site, all about feathers and feather magick.

# 6

## NATURE SPIRITS
## OF THE EARTH

Earth spirits are solid by the nature of their element. They most prefer to emerge after dark. They live close to the earth, forests, or in mounds or hillocks and adopt the colour and substance of leaves or plants. Their role is to protect the trees, sacred sites, minerals, land, and plants.

In a forested area, there may be an unusual number of faery doors in a group of trees, all at different levels with creeper walkways between trees. When I was in the Green Mountains in Queensland, Australia, on the midwinter solstice in 2011, the forest was alive with sounds and rustling though there was no wind. Seasonal transitions are times when faery doors become visible everywhere.

### The Nature of Earth Spirits

Some earth spirits may be friendly and gentle to humans, guiding them if lost and conveying healing powers through herbs, trees, and flowers. In modern times, however, when people may be more careless about the environment, these spirits can display a fiercer side. They are part of the powerful energies of soil, grass, trees, mountains, and plants, and earth spirits especially resent the squandering of resources.

# Children and Earth Spirits

Children have a special affinity with earth spirits. Anna, who is now fifteen and lives in Sundsvall in northern Sweden, described to me how when she was five or six she would regularly see and talk to gnomes near a stream close to her home. There were two couples, each about as high as her knees. The men, one older than the other, had white beards and wore pointed hats and green clothes. There were two women gnomes in green dresses and two small children gnomes. Once a local boy asked Anna to whom she was talking and she replied "to the little people." He told her she was crazy, and so she never talked to the gnomes again.

## Earth-Spirit Associations

**Archetypal elemental spirit:** gnome

**Earth-spirit ruler:** Geb or Ghob, an elemental king whose throne is covered with crystals, silver, and gold. He is especially guardian of miners and others who work within the earth. Also ruled by Galadriel, elven queen of the earth faeries made famous in J. R. R. Tolkien's *Lord of the Rings*.

**Favourite time of day:** midnight

**Favourite season:** winter

**Energy:** receptive/passive

**Earth-spirit characteristic:** facilitator/carer

**Earth-spirit elemental tool:** pentacle

**Earth-spirit ritual substance:** salt

**Favourite colours:** green or golden brown

**Psychic gifts they offer:** psychometry/clairsentience

**Polarity:** Goddess

**Earth-spirit energy-raiser:** drumming

**Deities:** earth mothers, creator goddesses, mistress of animals and crone/wise women goddesses; also earth fathers, horned gods, and gods of the hunt

**Archangel:** Uriel, Archangel of Protection and the earth, who protects it with his torch of fire

**Earth-spirit crystals:** most agates (especially moss and tree agate), amazonite, aventurine, boulder opal, emerald, fossils, jet, malachite, petrified or fossilized wood, rose quartz, rutilated quartz, smoky quartz, red and gold tiger's eye, and all stones with holes in the centre

**Earth-spirit animals and birds:** antelope, badger, bear, boar, cow, bull, dog, kangaroo, stag, sheep, squirrel, rabbit, chipmunk, serpent, snake, bee, spider, wombat, wallaby, and wolf

**Ailments and body parts especially healed by earth spirits: :** legs, feet, spine, skeleton, bowels, teeth, and genitals

**Sense:** touch, taste, and common sense

**Earth-spirit fragrances:** cypress, fern, geranium, heather, hibiscus, honeysuckle, magnolia, oakmoss, patchouli, sagebrush, sweetgrass, tea tree, vervain, and vetivert

**Positive qualities/strengths offered by earth spirits:** patience, stability, generosity, reliability, endurance, perseverance, respect for others and traditions, protectiveness, fertility (also given by water spirits), acceptance of others as they are and of self, groundedness, tolerance, and caring for the environment

**Less-desirable qualities:** over caution, rigidity, unwillingness to adapt, blinkered vision, stubbornness, laziness, greed, inertia, and materialism

**Earth-spirit places:** caves, crop circles, crypts, fields, forests, ice, snow, rocks, hills and mountains, gardens, mines, rocks, old stone circles and homes, and near ley or psychic power lines

**Materials for attracting earth spirits:** salt, herbs, flowers, trees, coins, bread, corn and wheat, fabrics, nuts, clay, grass, soil, berries, potpourri, crystals and gems, plants, and sand

**Astrological signs:** Capricorn, Virgo, and Taurus

**Planets:** Venus and Saturn

**Empowerment to call the power of the earth spirits:** "Earth spirits, may I grow like the grain and the forests to give and receive abundance."

**Use earth-spirit magick for:** protection, property, the home and all domestic matters, stability in any area of your life, a steady infusion of money and banishing debt, families and animals, all environmental rituals, spells concerning institutions (such as law, politics, finance, health care, and education), famine, deforestation, land pollution, devastation through unwise building or industrialization, and caring for animals and their natural habitats.

## Earth Spirits and Earth Energies

Because ancient sacred sites—such as stone circles, ancient burial mounds, and ancient chambers—were created where subterranean ley energy lines or faery paths meet, the places have become meeting or dwelling places for earth spirits. Indigenous sites in native North America, aboriginal Australia, as well as other places of indigenous power are also rich in land energies.

The *korrs*, or *korreds*, male Breton earth spirits with huge heads, spiky hair, and dark, wrinkly faces, guard the ancient stones and stone circles. In Brittany, a region in the southwest of France, it is believed the korrs helped create the original sacred sites and that they still frighten away those who would desecrate the stones. Korrs specialise in metalwork and store their treasures in the ancient stone tables, especially at Carnac beneath numerous rows of small monoliths (standing stones); it is said to be impossible to count the treasures.[1] The day of the korrs is the first Wednesday in May.

From my own extensive research on ley energies, with the expert advice of Scottish scholar and earth energy researcher John Plowman, I discovered a number of earth-spirit legends along ley lines. For example, the east–west ley line that crosses the Isle of Wight (my own home area in southern England) eventually joins with Avebury. Near the centre of the island in Godshill is a major intermediate point on this ley. Godshill Church now stands on a steep hill; legend says that the original plan was to erect the church at the southwest corner of the village on the ley. On the first day, the stones were piled on the planned site and markers set. The next morning, the stones and pegs had been moved to the top of the hill and placed in position. Suspecting trickery, the bishop had the workmen restore the stones to the original site and placed guards at the end of the day to prevent any recurrence. At midnight the stones began to move of their own accord and rolled to the top of the hill, arranging themselves in the correct positions. The markers, too, placed themselves in the ground. The bishop accepted the will of God and consecrated the hilltop site, calling it God's Hill. In another version of the legend, faeries moved the stones because the original site was the site of their revels.[2]

Go to any old site as twilight is falling. Sit quietly for a while by the stones or in a grove of ancient trees and you will connect with the earth spirits and feel the throb of the earth beneath you.

## Exploring the World of the Earth Fey

At twilight, sit quietly in a meadow, grassy plain, or park where the grass is long.

- Half-close your eyes and tune in to sounds around you—the breeze rippling the grass, a bird's song, or the distant roar of traffic.

- In your mind, turn down the volume until you are sitting in a pool of silence.

- Through half-closed eyes, focus on a large clump of grasses and allow tiny faces and forms to take shape. Do not force this or try to analyse, as the logical mind will intrude.

- As the light fades and the grasses become less distinct, the forms may become more distinct, moving and swaying. Go with the rhythm, moving your upper body and arms very slightly to create harmony with the energy.

- Begin a soft, slow empowerment or chant to create a connection. Whenever you return to the place to call the fey, whisper it to the winds continuously, melodiously, and mesmerically. For example, "Blessed people of the green whispering grasses, come to me, be with me, share with me your blessings."

- Gradually become still and silent and you may slowly feel the withdrawing of the energies. When you are ready, get up and quietly move away.

- You can adapt the chant according to the place you are attempting to connect with the fey people.

- Turn just once as you leave and you may be rewarded with a fleeting glimpse of an earth spirit watching you.

## Nature-Spirit Places

Indigenous earth spirits, who have lived on land long before humans came, form a special affinity with particular humans who settle on the land. For example, the Nunnehi, "the people who live anywhere," indigenous Native American faeries, are associated with the Cherokee nation. It is told that they once lived beneath the sacred Niwaski Mound in North Carolina and under Blood Mountain at the head of Nottley River in Georgia. They assisted the people many times and some say guided the Cherokee to safety during the Indian resettlement (see chapter 2).

Another race of fey people who populated the same area, the Yûñwï Tsun-sdi, or "little people," who lived in rock caves on the mountainside. They are described as knee-high but good-looking adults with long hair falling almost to the ground. They danced and drummed and would guide lost travelers. During a severe smallpox outbreak among the east Cherokee, legend records how the Yûñwï Tsunsdi took a wandering sick man to their caves and cured him.[3]

## Forest and Woodland Spirits

We have all heard the wind and thought it was speaking or seen faces or figures in the trees. In Thailand, the legendary tree faeries are called Naree Pon or Makalipon. They are said to spring from the fruit of the nareepol trees as beautifully formed miniature women. It is told the Father God Phra Indra created the Himapan forest as a home for Prince Vessandara and his family and he planted sixteen magical nareepon trees that blossomed.

After four days, the bunches of tree faeries were to be formed, and they would sing and dance; after seven days they would shrivel to the size of a person's hand. They were created, it is said, to discover which deities were lustful, as those who made love with the tree women would fall into a coma and on awakening would have lost their divine powers. Certainly some petrified fruits do seem to resemble faeries, especially very ancient ones, and can be seen in the Wat Mahathat temple near Bangkok.

### Receiving Healing from the Tree Spirits

- Tree spirits are particularly receptive to healing. Choose a mature, healthy tree.

- If possible, work so that sunlight is filtering through the leaves.

- Begin by sitting with your back against the tree trunk for a few minutes, making connection with the forest floor.

- Put your hands on the forest floor, press down with your feet, and let any excess energies and negative feelings sink into the earth.

- When you feel calm, stand facing the tree so your fingers and toes are lightly touching the trunk.

• Draw up the rich, golden energy through your feet and legs and picture it as liquid gold flowing through every part of your body, finding its own pathways.

• Focus on any part of your body that is experiencing pain or problems and picture the energy swirling around the area, counterclockwise and then clockwise, clearing the blockage or problem.

• If your mind is troubled or you cannot rest, visualise the energy flowing in and out of your mind, clearing the tension and leaving peace and a sense of well-being.

• You may experience a surge of energy or a gentler flow of light within you. Continue creating the circuit with the tree-spirit energy until you feel powerful and protected.

• Turn around slowly so you are now standing with your back against the tree.

• Close your eyes and you may see the spirit in front of you.

• Hug the tree and tie biodegradable ribbons or flowers to its branches.

If you do not have time to visit a tree and you feel unwell, in time you will be able to visualise a particular tree you often work with as if it is in front of you and the golden energies will flow through you.

## Tree Mothers and Moss Wives

The moss or wood wives of Germany are friendly and helpful beings who assist and advise travelers and reward mortals they like with wood chips, splinters, and leaves that turn into gold. They can be very vulnerable to fiercer nature spirits or to humans who cut down their trees.

If anyone helps with tree conservation in the area, they may find a small, perfectly smooth piece of wood, a gift from the moss wives. If taken home and set on the hearth or in a warm place, it will attract prosperity to their home.

Unlike many other flower, plant, and tree spirits, moss wives live on maturing trees and will do so even if their tree dies.

## Meeting the Tree Mothers

Tree mothers are present in every woodland or forest in every land. You will find them in old trees with twisted shapes with quite distinctive features on the trunk. They are recognisable by a distinctive, older, wrinkled female face about the height of an ordinary face, and they appear as though the tree mother was standing against the trunk and in fact the trunk is her body. Her arms are formed from shortened branches.

Tree mothers are immensely comforting, and protective in the cold, lonely times. They are also challenging, like any tough mother pushing her reluctant offspring to ever greater achievements, personally and spiritually. Each offers the wisdom of the many ages through which she has lived; she may have moved to different trees over the millennia.

- To encounter a tree mother, visit a mature forest wherever you live. There will most likely be a number of tree mothers in a forest belonging to the same species.

- You will identify one most easily in a tree that is coiled with many offshoots or with leaves and creepers that wind around you, but not in a menacing manner.

- In warmer lands, you will find tree mothers in olive trees, date palms, Australian eucalyptus trees, orange trees, banyan trees, and other tropical trees that mature much earlier in warm climes. Tree mothers will reflect the climate and the soil that nurtures those trees, so a Mediterranean or Californian tree mother may be alternately fiery and expansive.

- In contrast, your mother of the northern steppes will have little time for pleasantries as she struggles to protect the roots from the ice and snow, but will uphold you in the most drear and dire situations and will give you great courage.

- There is usually a particular tree mother, maybe in your garden or local park or woodland, that almost instantly empowers and strengthens you whenever you feel sad or dispirited. As you work with the tree, the tree mother takes on the personality akin to a wise aunt or grandmother. Sit close to her, put your hands on her trunk, and tell her your troubles; you will feel instantly better.

## Finding Answers from the Tree Mothers

You can also gain direct wisdom from the tree mothers. You will need two or three trees at least, one of which should be a mother tree. They sometimes gather in twos or threes to gossip.

- Sit against the mother tree, choosing a day when there is a breeze. There does not need to be a fierce wind.

- First attune yourself to the time scale of the wind's natural dialogue with the trees—the wind gusting and catching up the leaves so they move suspended on their branches, then the silence as the leaves wait seemingly in anticipation for the next gust.

- Before asking a question, tune in to the rhythms of the voice of the leaves, which may speak in a lilt, in a staccato manner or a rush like a wave crashing on the shore.

- When you are attuned, speak your question to your tree mother and she will allow your question to be first taken up by the wind, which may have answers of its own, adding to the wisdom of the echoing leaves.

- It is the tree mother who will speak and her voice appears between gusts, as the leaves are still like a powerful whisper, strong as the crashing of the sea.

- Ask a second question, then a third and listen to the tree mother. Afterward, allow the leaves to add anything that is unsaid as the wind catches the leaves once more.

- Find a sheltered spot to scribble down what may be a series of seemingly unconnected words or a theme in which one word recurs. For example, *wait, seek,* or *forgive.*

- When you return home, arrange or rearrange the phrases and you may find they relate not only to the questions asked but also to general issues; they could be simple suggestions for how your life could progress.

- Once you have worked with the wind and the leaves several times, you can hear the tree mother, even on a windless day, with the same deep throaty whisper.

## Dwellers under or Close to the Earth

### Gnomes

Found in much of northern and western Europe and Scandinavia and taken by settlers to Australia, New Zealand, the United States, and Canada, gnomes are, along with dwarves, the most common form of earth spirit. They live underground in deep forests for up to a thousand years. Many are great metal workers and spend time in their underground forges. They have wives and families and are all very strong.

Gnomes found in gardens (both private and public) are slightly more sociable, though they are attached to the plants and wildlife and not to the owners of the land. They vary in size from two to three feet and resemble garden gnome statues though generally are browner and more gnarled.

Males usually have a peaked rather than pointed red caps and wear blue or green with boots made from birch bark. Females wear green and often have head scarves. The gnomes may or may not have white beards. The name may be derived from *ge-nomos,* which translates as "earth dweller."

Gnomes care for the earth, minerals, metals, plants, and wild animals. Gnomes are very similar to dwarves in appearance, but are slightly smaller and more graceful and can run quickly for their size.

Forest gnomes live in the darkest part of the forest, often close to caves, and make their homes within trees. They avoid contact with humans as they fear humans will steal their treasure.

Garden gnomes most often live in older gardens or cultivated land and are great herbalists. A resident gnome will attract luck and prosperity to your home and encourage plants to flourish. They do not usually mix with the house spirits and they will come and go as they please.

## *Attracting a Gnome to Your Garden*

You can attract a gnome wherever you live; I have even known people with a balcony that has a gnome as a resident. However, gnomes will not live indoors. To attract the favour of gnomes, if possible buy a plain brown or grey pottery gnome figure. Work just with one initially. You can create a gnomery later if you wish and your garden will positively blossom.

- Set the figure in a sheltered shady spot.

- Leave it for three weeks (gnome magick is slow acting and you may need to wait for a gnome to come along). If you already have a resident gnome, he will greatly love this statue and you will sense activity in terms of vibrant growth around the statue.

- If you can see plant life springing around the figure and (more importantly) feel a steady throbbing energy, like someone treading the earth down, you know a gnome has adopted your statue as a temporary residence.

- Be patient and add another gnome figure or two, perhaps a small family if nothing seems to be happening. Gnomes also like small ponds.

- When you sense a gnome in one of the statues, set a small bowl with a lid (the kind used for sugar or jam) in front of it. Only work with one statue even if you have a number of them.

- In the evening, put an earth-spirit crystal such as an agate (see Earth-Spirit Associations earlier in this chapter) and a coin in the pot and replace the lid.

- If you have a question about a practical or financial arrangement in your life or your home, ask the gnome. Gnomes are very slow thinkers but very wise and so you may have to wait a while, several days or even a week, before you see a sign in the natural world that will answer your question. You will know because the sign will be something unusual and the answer will flood your mind.

- Add a coin every day but only ask one question a week maximum and go and thank the gnome when you get an answer.

- When the pot is full, bury three of the coins and the crystal beneath the gnome and use the rest of the money towards basic foodstuff or start a savings account. Though they love gems, gnomes err on the side of financial carefulness. Gnomes do not like mortals feeding them so give food to the garden birds instead.

- Over the weeks, you will find that money flow slowly improves and that the outflow is slowing in your personal finances. Gnomes have a psychological effect, even on shopaholics like myself.

- Leave the daily coin, even if you don't sense gnome energy on a particular day. One day you will discover your gnome and maybe his family have moved on, but by that point you will have absorbed his wisdom and common sense.

# Dwarves

Dwarves are first described in ancient Egypt, the most famous being Bes. He assisted in childbirth; brought good luck; and protected the home, children, and pregnant women; and brought peaceful sleep. Though not an attractive figure (with a huge head, prominent tongue and genitals, bow legs, and a lion's or cat's ears, mane, and tail), he was entirely benign to those whom he guarded against malevolent spirits, serpents, and general misfortune. He wore a lion or panther skin. When women were in childbirth, Bes was depicted brandishing knives or playing loud instruments to drive away all harm.

## Invoking the Protection of Bes

Use a red candle, spice incense, a bowl of soil, and a piece of paper to work ritually with Bes. Your ritual can be for protection of home and family; for all matters concerning babies, children, and mothers; to increase pleasure and skill in dancing, singing, and music; to bring joy; and for courage in the face of opposition. Tuesday is an especially good day for Bes magick.

- Draw or trace this image of Bes on a strip of paper and next to it write the protection or gifts you need in four or five words, such as, *Bes, protector, make me brave.*

- Now light a red candle; from the candle's flame, light a spicy incense stick and write the same empowerment in the air in incense stick smoke over the picture. Write the empowerment three times.

- Return the incense stick to its holder and set light to the strip of paper, dropping it as it catches light into a bowl of soil, repeating the empowerment three times.

- Leave the candle and incense to burn through and bury the paper in the soil, whether it burned totally or went out beneath a growing plant or tree, repeating the empowerment three more times.

## Traditional Dwarves

Traditional dwarves are widespread and most common in Germany (especially in the Black Forest and Harz Mountains), Scandinavia, Switzerland, and other countries settled by western Europeans.

Dwarves are small, wrinkled, and grey-bearded even when they are young because they mature at three years old. They have quite big heads, are shorter than humans (the height of a small child), but are very broad, sturdy, and strong.

Dwarves leave their families at an early age to live in bands or alone. They must stay out of sunlight which will turn them to stone, so they stay underground, in thick forests, or in dark rocky places during the day. They often prefer mountainous areas.

Like gnomes, dwarves mine for gems, minerals, and precious metals which they fiercely guard. They are famed for forging magical weapons and also beautiful jewelry.

In Scandinavia, dwarves fashioned the father god Odin's magical spear (*gungnir*) and the hammer of the thunder god Thor (*mjollnir*). The mjollnir is said to have always returned to Thor's hand after it had reached its target (usually against his enemies, the frost giants). For themselves and those they favoured such as the hero Siegfried, the dwarves created helmets, incredibly light chain mail, and metallic cloaks to make the wearer invisible.

In Norse cosmology, four of the strongest dwarves Norðri, Suðri, Austri, and Vestr, (northern, southern, eastern, and western) held the four corners of the heavens on their shoulders, thus giving their names to the four directions.

## Nibelungen

The *Nibelungen* are another kind of dwarf found in Germany, Norway, and Denmark. They live in a deep underground palace made of pure crystals. Nibelungen work in gold and are famed for their magical gold rings that grant invisibility and contain great power that can be used for good or evil.

At night, the Nibelungen enter the forests. If they are feeling bad-tempered, which they often are, they lure travelers with hoards of gold that disappear the second a mortal touches them. On a really bad dwarf day, they leave false trails to lure humans from their path into thick forest where they become hopelessly lost.

The Nibelungen's gold is guarded by the dragon named Fafnir in their absence (see chapter 7 on fire spirits).

# Mining Spirits

The older the mining tradition the greater the mine-spirit lore. Mine-spirit lore exists anywhere that mining activities take place, from Cornwall in the west of England, through Wales, Germany, Scandinavia, and the Andes regions in South America. They have been identified from the first mining activities in neolithic times with antler picks.

Mine spirits have a long tradition of most often being helpful and occasionally life saving, but in some lands such as Bolivia and Russia the mine spirit can take on a more sinister aspect if not appeased. Mining spirits may take on remarkably similar appearance to the miners they protect. The sturdy dwarf-like blue caps are so named because the flat caps they wear are like those of the miners. Traditionally, blue caps helped push heavy trucks of coal in the northern and midland English mines when mining was a major industry in the area. They are described as dusty and very small, but strong, and would help a tired miner fill his cart before disappearing into the blackness. Unlike other mine spirits, the blue caps would expect small coins to be left each day on the rock at the end of a shift and no miner would pick these up.

## Knockers

These are Cornish dwarflike spirits that dwell in the old tin mines, especially around the mysterious misty Bodmin Moor in Cornwall in southwest England. Bodmin Moor has strong traditions with Arthurian legends; it is home to many longstanding stones and dolmens (stone burial chambers). Tin mining began in Cornwall in 2100 BCE and the last mine closed at South Crofty between Camborne and Redruth in 1998.

Even as mining declines in many parts of the world, mine spirits are still heard tapping underground, especially the knockers on Bodmin Moor. When the mines were still open, the knockers tapped to tell miners where there was a rich vein of ore or if there was danger. There are many stories of how the knockers would guide trapped miners to safety by their tapping. In return, miners would leave food for the knockers.

## Coblynau

These are the spirits of the Welsh coal and gold mines, described as eighteen inches tall and dressed in miner's overalls and helmets with tiny picks and lanterns. Like the knockers, they cared for their miners in return for tributes of food and drink. Various tales tell of shoulder taps leading rescuers to an unconscious miner.[4]

According to the Reverend Edmund Jones of Tranch, Newport in 1813, the coblynau also had their own mines. He described how William Evans from Hafodafel passed a faery coal mine while crossing the Beacon Mountain very early one morning, though there was no mortal mine in the area. He saw faeries cutting coal, filling sacks, and lifting the full sacks on to horses in total silence.[5]

## Tio

During pre-Hispanic times in the highland mines of Bolivia, benign earth spirits or *huacas* were considered under the protection of Pachamama, the earth goddess. Later, our Lady of the Mineshaft, a name for the Virgin Mary, replaced the old earth goddess as benign protector. Miners today invoke protection from the Virgin Mary or Our Lady of the Mineshaft against hostile male and female earth-demon spirits. El Tio is the mountain spirit, also called Huay or Supay. In Peru he is called Muqui. El Tio is Spanish for "uncle"; an icon of El Tio is placed in every Bolivian mine as the protector, though his lore was mixed with the Christian devil concept. He is either pictured as blond and bearded or a clay figure and is placed in a niche in the miner's work area in every active mineshaft. All have a lump of metal in the centre linked to the metal being sought in the mine. They all have horns, and the eyes are usually made of discarded light bulbs from miners' helmets and the teeth of shards of crystals or glass. The mouth is open for a lighted cigarette and cocoa to chew, and his hands are open to receive alcohol. He must be appeased or he gets hungry and angry. Tuesdays, Fridays, and especially during the month of August involve special offerings (or *ch'alla*) to El Tio.

## Working with Mine Spirits for Prosperity and Bringing Out Talents

- Saturdays are good for fey-metal magick.

- Choose any metal associated with the fey.

- Use copper for growth or improvement in any matter.

- Use silver for gentler energies to develop talents you have abandoned or never fully evolved.

- Use gold for fast-moving success, fame, or wealth.

- Use tin for retaining or regaining prosperity after injustice.

- Use bronze, an alloy of copper and tin, for combining two careers or making a career out of a talent.

- Use coins of the appropriate colour or tin coins at museums or antique shops.

- Alternatively use earrings, links from necklaces, bracelets, chains, or charms.

- Bronze Chinese divinatory coins with holes in the middle are especially lucky.

- Keep a box of different small metal items from garage sales. Avoid iron or steel.

- You will need three pieces of your chosen metal, a ceramic plate, a small bowl of salt, and a large bowl containing soil to represent the treasures of the earth. The pieces of metal could be different.

- Light a blue candle and place the first piece of your chosen metal on the plate. Rest the plate on the soil saying, "Spirits of the earth, you who bring treasures from deep within the earth bring me [name what you want] by [name your desired time scale]."

- Scatter a circle of salt around the bowl of earth and repeat the words. Make the circle clockwise regardless of the hemisphere in which you live.

- Set the plate on the bowl of earth and the second piece of metal on the plate. Scatter a second circle of salt outside the first circle (clockwise), again repeating the words.

- Take the third piece of metal and set that on the plate. Scatter a third circle of salt outside the second (again, clockwise). Repeat the chant.

- Now pass the plate above the candle flame clockwise nine times, each time saying, "Spirits of the earth, you who bring the treasures from deep within the earth, I thank you for your blessings soon to be received and I will do good for the earth and all its creatures."

- Leave the metal on the plate resting on the bowl of earth overnight and let the candle burn out. In the morning, set the metal in a leather purse or cloth drawstring bag and carry it as a talisman.

- Place the pouch on the plate resting on the soil overnight every Saturday to recharge the energies until the result is achieved.

## The Trooping Spirits of the Earth

Many faeries live in troops or bands, a number of which are described in chapter 4. Trooping faeries are generally small with insectlike wings.

### Abatwa

Said to be the tiniest fey creatures in existence, the Abatwa are very elusive and only reveal themselves to children under the age of four, magical practitioners, clairvoyants, and pregnant women. If a woman in her seventh month of pregnancy sees an abatwa, the sex of the abatwa will be the same as the unborn child.

Abatwa are perfect miniatures of the members of the African tribes in their region, and their clan and family structures are similar, especially to the Zulu nation. The original Abatwa were aboriginal Twa and Bushmen (or *Bosjesmans*), the primordial inhabitants of Rwanda and Burundi.

Their complex dwellings are far deeper than anthills, though they coexist with ants and may sometimes ride ants. Legend says that their dwellings have elaborate paintings on the walls and mosaic floors made of seeds and packed sand. On their semiannual hunts, they kill small animals with tiny poison-tipped arrows. The rest of the time, they eat plants and seeds and are great ecologists. Though smaller, these aboriginal African people resemble Australian aboriginal Mimi (see page 44).

## Svart, Dark, or Earth Elves

Dark or earth elves are found in troops in western Europe, especially in Germany, the Netherlands, and Scandinavia. Dark elves are skilled metalworkers, shoemakers, and spinners, even according to Grimm's faery stories about spirits spinning straw into gold. Dark elves are among the larger trooping spirits and are black or dark brown.[6] Like dwarves, dark elves do not come out by the light of day or they will be turned into stone.

Mound elves, a subgroup of the dark or earth elves, can be helpful or malicious according to whim. They live above ground near ancient burial mounds or sacred sites in dark forests like the Black Forest in Germany. In the Black Forest, a fearsome elf king leads them. He is called Erlkonig or Erl, and is also known as Ellerkonge in Denmark. He was made famous by Goethe's poem written in 1782. The elf king was notorious for abducting children and appeared to warn people of their impending death and its manner. Around the time of Goethe's poem, child mortality was common and so the elf king became a scapegoat for the sudden death of an infant.[7]

In some German folk tales elves were no more than a foot high and naked or dressed in rags and were seen as mischievous young boys, also found in English folk tales.

## Pixies

Though pixies, or *piskies*, are small, dark-winged Cornish elves from the southwest of England, they have also been reported in mainland Europe. Like other Celtic nature spirits, the pixies traveled to many different parts of the world with settlers. Once said to be Picts, a fierce race of warriors, they have apparently continued to diminish in size till one day they will disappear. However, they are very brave and ingenious; when they migrate to other lands, they will fight indigenous spirits for territory.

In Cornwall some pixies live on land and others make their homes close to the sea between the high- and low-water marks of the tide. Said to be no larger than a human hand in their natural size, they are shape-shifters who can increase or decrease their size. Pixies are tricksters, stealing horses at night to ride them across the moor, twisting and tangling the manes. Pixies also lead humans in circles using the powers of illusion to create and cause paths to disappear, calling down patches of mist alternated by dazzling sunshine, calling up lights at night to indicate houses that are not there and making marshland appear solid.

## Protecting Yourself from Earth-Spirit Mischief

It can be wonderful to watch small dark figures scurrying or dancing around an ancient site at night, to hear faint elven music in the distance, or to hear whisperings in the grass. Occasionally, however, you may encounter a less-friendly presence, often later in the evening or in a lonely place.

- No fey form, except for the Breton korrs, likes iron. Carry a small iron nail or two along with some iron pyrites or Fool's Gold in a little purse as protection when out at night in lonely places.

- When camping or caravanning, put iron inside the doorway to stop mischievous intruders. Open the purse and set the nails either side of the tent door and the iron pyrites against the back flap.

- As long as iron is in the purse as you journey and you have a friendly presence, earth spirits will not bother you.

- Do not sleep overnight too close to old sites. There will be a great deal of fey energy, not necessarily malevolent but which may disturb you and give you bad dreams.

- If you are in a deep forest or walking in the hills and sense a less-than-welcoming presence or hear muttering rather than whispering, switch on a flashlight.

- Don't run; the little people will enter the spirit of the hunt and will chase you and maybe lead you astray by creating mist and mirages. You are more powerful, but even small earth spirits can turn into bullies if they sense fear.

- Holding the flashlight, turn around counterclockwise nine times and say the ancient Celtic anti-malevolent fey spell three times. This spell was once spoken by midwives blessing new infants with three drops of water on the brow to represent the protection of earth, sky, and sea.
  *"To aid thee from the feys,*
  *To guard thee from the host,*
  *To aid thee from the gnome,*
  *To shield thee from the spectre,*
  *To keep thee for the three,*
  *To shield thee and surround thee."*

In the next chapter, we will work with the vibrant and dynamic spirits of the fire.

Chapter 6 Sources

1. http://www.megalithia.com/brittany/carnac/

2. Eason, Cassandra. *Ghost Encounters.* Worcestershire: Blandford Books, 2008.

3. Yûñwï Tsunsdi, http://www.fl-wolf-clan.org/littlepeople.htm

4. Sikes, Wirk. *British Goblins:Welsh Folklore, Fairy Mythology, Legends, and Traditions.* Forgotten Books, 2010.

5. Sikes, Wirk. *British Goblins:Welsh Folklore, Fairy Mythology, Legends, and Traditions.* Forgotten Books, 2010.

6. Zelinsky, Paul O., and the Brothers Grimm. *Rumplestiltskin.* New York: Puffin, 1996.

7. *The Erl King* (song). Words by Goethe with the new translation by Fox Strangways, A. H. and S. Wilson, written by Johann Karl Gottfried Loewe. Oxford University Press, 1935.

# 7

# NATURE SPIRITS
# OF THE FIRE

Fire spirits are the most volatile, unpredictable, and unsociable to humans and yet are the most exciting of the nature spirits. They are fierce, elusive, and untameable, shimmering in the blazing heat of the noonday sun, flickering in flames, flaring sparklike from bonfires or generating their own fire like the dragon. A fire spirit will absorb the power of any fire it encounters and grow temporarily larger, more dynamic, and more potent. But because they are made of balls of energy or light, fire spirits tend to be far shorter-lived than other elemental nature forms. The smaller, less-structured ones literally burn themselves out.

Fire spirits are of immense magical value as light bringers. They will give you the sudden courage or confidence to take the lead, believe in yourself and your own worth, demand what is reasonable, overcome injustice, speak your mind, and even clear away what you no longer need. Above all they inspire us to reach out to fulfil major dreams and ambitions.

Fire beings vary in size and intensity from mighty dragons to tiny but powerful, often unnamed fire faeries. Fire faeries live mainly outdoors and draw close to any bonfire, but they might also be seen indoors in the hearth fire or wood-burning stove when winter in the northern climes is at its deepest. Though they may cause a sudden rush of flame or sparks, they will not stay long. They may also manifest as fireflies and glow worms in caves. Fire spirits, commonly called earth lights, dance over sacred sites, areas of volcanic activity, or where there are subterranean earth movements. Even the fey forms of fire spirits are not pretty dancing faeries, but dynamos that will light up your world and ignite your inner fire.

## Working Safely with Fire Spirits

- Keep a water crystal, such as green or purple fluorite or green jade, close to your workspace. If you feel you are getting too hot emotionally or physically, hold it in your dominant hand.

- Before beginning any fire-spirit work, splash your hairline, the centre of your brow, your throat, and both of your wrist pulse points with cool water. These are the easiest places on your body to access your higher chakras and energy centres. The wrists link you to the gentle, healing heart chakra. Say, "May only goodness and light enter me and protect me. I welcome the spirits of the fire, but do not burn too fiercely, I ask with respect."

- Splash yourself with water in the same way after the ritual and say, "I thank the spirits of the fire who have filled me with light and inspiration, and may their goodness and light remain in my life. Return now to your own element with blessings."

### Fire-Spirit Magical Associations
**Archetypal elemental spirit:** salamander

**Fire-spirits ruler:** Djinn, a being made of pure fire, a glorious flame-like creature with flashing ruby eyes who is never still and rules all fire spirits

**Favourite time of day:** noon

**Favourite season:** summer

**Energy:** active and projective

**Fire-spirit characteristic**: creator and action

**Elemental tool:** wand

**Fire-spirit ritual substance:** candle

**Favourite colours:** red, gold, or orange

**Psychic gifts they offer:** clairvoyance and connecting with
spirits and ghosts

**Polarity:** God

**Fire-spirit energy-raiser:** dance, ritual fires

**Deities:** fire gods and goddesses, deities of passion and seduction,
blacksmith and metal deities, and deities of the sun

**Archangel:** Michael, Archangel of the Sun, leader of all the great warrior
angels. The traditional dragon slayer with golden wings, red-and-gold
armour, and the scales of justice.

**Fire-spirit crystals:** amber, bloodstone, Boji stones, carnelian, dragon's
eggs, garnet, lava, iron pyrites, hematite, obsidian, ruby, and topaz

**Fire-spirit animals and birds:** cat, lion, cougar, stag, dragons, fireflies,
dragonflies, and the legendary golden phoenix. The phoenix, which
burns itself on a funeral pyre every five hundred years only to rise
again golden from the ashes, is a symbol of transformation and rebirth.

**Fire-spirit fragrances:** allspice, angelica, basil, bay, carnation, cedar-
wood, chamomile, cinnamon, cloves, copal, dragon's blood, frankin-
cense, heliotrope, juniper, lime, marigold, nutmeg, orange, rosemary,
and tangerine

**Ailments and body parts especially healed by fire spirits:**
heart, liver, spleen, and stomach ailments

**Sense:** vision, survival

**Positive qualities/strengths offered by fire spirits:** courage, inspiration, idealism, altruism, fidelity, perfectionism, defense of the weak, intuition, imagination, creativity, leadership, good health, transformation, fertility in all aspects of life (also earth and water spirits), mysticism, clairvoyance, prophecy, determination to overcome obstacles, energy, living spirit, and abundance

**Less-desirable qualities:** addiction (also earth spirits), anger, aggressiveness, cruelty, domination, hatred, jealousy, rebellion, being led by passion, flirtatious, unfaithful, and violence

**Fire-spirit places:** family hearth, deserts, shimmering sand, hilltop beacons, red rock formations, altars with candles, ritual and hearth fires, stars (sometimes also associated with air), bonfires, comets, rainbows, meteors, lightning torches (wood was believed to contain fire that could be released by friction), volcanoes, forest fires, and solar eclipses

**Materials for attracting fire spirits:** candles, beeswax, flames, ash, fibre-optic lamps, lightning, faery lights, flashlight beams swirled around in the darkness, jack o' lanterns, clear crystal spheres, gold, mirrors, oranges, suncatchers, sunflowers and all golden flowers

**Astrological signs:** Aries, Leo, and Sagittarius

**Planets:** the sun and Mars

**Empowerment to call the power of the fire spirits:**
"May I flame and flare and rise high to fulfill my dreams."

**Use fire-spirit magick for:** fulfilling ambitions, prosperity, justice, career advancement, wisdom in power and leadership, all creative and artistic ventures, fame, religion and spirituality, success in sports and competitive games, courage, to increase psychic powers (especially higher ones such as channelling pleasure, passion, and the consummation of love), for sacred sex, the removal of what is no longer needed, binding and banishing, protection against a vicious attack or threats, against drought and pollution, and with candle magick.

# Discovering Spirits of the Flames

## Salamanders

Salamanders are the legendary spirit fire lizards originally described as being from the Middle East, recorded most frequently in desert places. The larger the source of fire, the greater their size and power, though generally they are about a foot in length.[1]

Salamanders appear often as elongated wandlike faery beings in the shape of flames. Though salamanders live in volcanoes or lakes of fire, you can see them in large wood-burning bonfires. Like their earthly cousins, the chameleon, salamanders are constantly changing colour and perpetually moving like flame itself within fire, especially tall conflagrations such as festival fires.

Salamanders can also manifest on sand shimmering in sunlight along the shore of an inland lake or the sea, resembling large, golden, upright lizards that come in and out of vision like a mirage. They can also be found in sandy inland places in bright sunlight where ordinary lizards sleep or dart around in shimmering heat. In a forest fire, they may burn black near the base of the fire.

I first saw spirit salamanders on the sandy shore at a huge French lake called La Sidillaille in central France. The sun was illuminating the sand crystals and creating mist mirages. On the sand were dozens of actual small lizards, darting and disappearing under rocks only to reappear. The spirit-fire salamanders resembled larger, darting, rainbow-flickering, flamelike creatures and would dematerialise if stared at. Because I had a huge personal transformation to make when I returned to England, it seemed especially apt I should have seen them as I sat wrestling with my decision.

Occasionally, salamanders become beautiful dancing females with lizard-like eyes and flaming hair. In an Australian aboriginal myth, the salamanders, or "sleepy lizard women," made their camp on what became Uluru, previously known as Ayers Rock, the sacred red hill that rose from the ashes after the camp of the sleepy lizard women was burned.

In the Middle East, it is believed that djinns, or fire genies, also take the form of lizards and may ask for the help of mortals in this form. If help is granted, the humans are richly rewarded.

## Working with Salamander Power

There are two ways you can work with salamander power wherever you live.

### Summer / Hot-Place Energies

Sites include sandy lake sides or islands; rocky places on a sunny day; year-round hot locations like the Mediterranean lands, the Middle East, Indonesia, or India. Alternatively, work when sunbeams are bouncing off a large expanse of water. Find a place where there are real lizards, or use the sun shining to create a haze to allow your mind and your eyes to create tall, beautiful, golden, dancing lizard women.

- Sit or kneel and call the salamander energies to enrich or transform your life with this very old song of the salamanders. I do not know its source, but I was taught it some years ago by an old healer friend who lived in Almeria in Spain and loved the golden sand lizards on the shore. Softly and continuously recite the call aloud or in your mind, singing it to a simple tune if you wish and swaying slightly, as if in time with the visualised salamander women: "Salamanders of gold, lizard women of the sun, flame bright and illumine my world. Flare and sparkle, radiant ones, dance through the days of sunlight and through my life that I may dance gloriously with you, salamanders of the sun."

- When you feel filled with joy and power, let the image of the golden salamander women fade from your mind, but dig the sand or bury your feet in it as you walk. If you are working through visualisation, picture the sand soft and golden and gradually allow your feet to return to the place where you are working. In this way, you will continue to draw the warmth and optimism into yourself.

• Create your own alternative salamander call if you wish to take on a transformation in any area of life.

## Winter / Cooler-Place Energies

Because fey energies exist on the etheric or spirit plane, you can work with any spirit forms in any location. You just need stronger visualisation. Because salamanders are fire creatures, any fire source will evoke their presence.

• Work with a tall outdoor bonfire, an indoor hearth, or a stove fire where you can clearly see the base of the fire. The salamanders will be smaller in the indoor fires, but just as powerful.

• For both indoor and outdoor rituals, you will need to picture your salamanders as graceful, dancing wandlike beings of flame moving in the colours of the fire.

• Identify a group of dancing salamanders. As you sit, sway your hands and body so you connect with their flickering movement.

• Recite the salamander call above as you watch your salamanders. When you have finished, build up the fire in thanks.

## Safely Closing Any Salamander Contact

Salamanders will only work with you for a very short time and will remain in a fire no longer than the fire lasts.

• Limit any salamander contact (even when done on sandy sunlit shores) to about five or ten minutes.

• Afterward, always thank them and wish them well and ask them to go in peace back to their realms. Their energies buzzing unchecked may make you feel restless or irritable and less cautious and safety conscious than usual.

- Always leave them first and leave the fire burning safely or the sunny place you visualised them so that the salamanders can return to the fire source at the time of their choosing.

## Jinn/Djinn

Jinn are called "the wish granters." Nevertheless, they are the tricksters of the universe and need to be handled with respect and caution.[2] According to myth, jinn are formed from smokeless fire and were created thousands of years before Adam and ruled by kings, the last of whom, Jân ibn Jân, was credited with building the pyramids. However, because they would not obey divine law (due to their wild and unpredictable nature as fire spirits), they were driven into exile by the angels and lost their immortality and their benign nature to humanity. The angels cast shooting stars at them from the heavens and their nature also causes fights among them that can result in their destruction.

Good jinn are beautiful while evil jinn are huge, ugly, and can cause sand-storms. Jinn are natural magicians and shape-shifters who travel with the speed of light. Their natural home is in the Emerald Mountains of Kâf; how-ever, they appear almost anywhere, especially in bottles or lamps as genies as I describe later.

It was once believed by mediaeval magicians that with the use of talismans or magic, jinn could be forced to obey and give knowledge of the future, which they learned from eavesdropping on the angels in the lower heavens. In the Middle East, the jinn are linked in modern times with the desert campfires of the Bedouin tribes and are invisible, except to children and wise men and women.

While I was researching a book on ancient Egyptian magick in Cairo, I got to know a man who made perfumes whose family was originally nomadic Bedouin. He had witnessed both jinns and magical salamanders as a child, and his grandmother, the tribal wise woman, saw them as well.

In the Old Testament, King Solomon had a magick ring with which he summoned jinns to help his armies win battles. Solomon was a master magician whose wisdom came from the secret book of the angel Raziel.

## Genies

"Genie" is the Westernised term for the jinn whose tradition has come from the stories of the Arabian knights and Aladdin and his wonderful lamp whose indwelling genie granted wishes.[3] This story reflected a common folk belief that centred especially on the old-fashioned, saucerlike oil lamps. The user of such a magick lamp had to be very careful what was requested, as the genie would take the wish literally. Also, the number of wishes was limited, after which the genie was free. Then he could turn against the owner of the lamp if the owner had been unwise with his or her wishes or unkind to the genie.

There is another related tradition more prevalent in the Westernised world of the spirit being contained in a sealed bottle.

## How to Cast Genie Bottle Spells Without Being Overwhelmed or Deluded

*Genie Wishes*

I am certainly not recommending you try summoning and controlling jinns, as it might be psychologically unsettling. However you can safely and positively use the symbolism of the genie in the bottle to concentrate your own wish power.

What you are bottling is not a spirit, rather your own powerful inner abilities to make your own wishes come true. You can strengthen that inner fire by using an external fire source, in this case either a red candle or a small oil lamp.

- Find an old bottle with a cork or screw-top lid. It should be made of dark glass. It can be a well-cleaned old beer bottle (we don't want inebriated genies) or even a stone bottle, the sort used for country cider. The bottle need only be small.

• Light the red candle and hold the open bottle in front of it so the flame shines through or on it.

• Add a pinch of salt to the open bottle for spiritual purification and say, "May my wishes bring joy to others as well as to myself."

• Move the bottle close to you. Holding it with both hands, move it to your lips and whisper your dearest wish or dream into the bottle.

• Put the cork in or screw the top on.

• Again, hold the bottle in front of the flame (not too near so it will get hot, but just so the light shines into or on it).

• Repeat, "May my wishes bring joy to others as well as to myself."

• Once again, set the bottle in front of the candle in the same manner.

• Thank the powers of fire and ask that you may remain inspired and focused to fulfil your dream.

• Blow out the candle and picture the fire entering the bottle.

• Splash yourself with cool water and put the bottle in a dark place where it will not be disturbed.

• Keep the extinguished candle wrapped and safe.

• If you lose sight of your dream, you can take the bottle out and relight the red candle in front of the bottle.

• Repeat your whispered wish into the candle flame but do not open the bottle. Blow out the candle.

• After three months, open the bottle, thank the fire essence and relight the candle. After a few minutes, wash out the bottle with water and leave it uncorked.

• Leave the candle to burn through to reabsorb the genie power.

- You can repeat the actions with a new candle and recork the bottle
  any time if your wish is slow in coming to fruition.

## The Power of the Dragons

Dragons are another archetypal fire spirit. Oriental dragons are associated mainly with the air and water. They rise in the spring and fight or mate, creating welcome rain. It is believed that as they do so they scatter fireballs and pearls of healing onto the earth and that these fireballs causes growth of magical healing herbs in the places they land.

The Scandinavian and Germanic/European dragons are, in contrast, the true fire-breathing dragons. They guard treasure, as chronicled in the Anglo-Saxon epic poem "Beowulf" thought to be written sometime between the eighth and eleventh century CE in England.[4] In almost every dragon story, the dragon guards gold within a deep cave. This is highly symbolic. In various magical traditions, gold was considered the most precious gift of the earth and was associated with the earth mother's life blood. As humans mined gold and other precious minerals more and more, they were depleting the goodness of the earth faster than it could be replaced, a process that takes millions of years. The dragons were trying to stop this. The dragon slayers were of course benefiting from the dragon gold hoards—and rarely gave it to the poor.

Magically, too, the treasure of the fire dragons represents creativity and spiritual wisdom and can be easily accessed with respect, although dragons can be invoked to attract resources for a particular worthwhile, practical, or monetary purpose, whether to travel or to launch a business or creative venture.

Dragons also symbolise the ability to overcome huge obstacles or odds through their stored fire power that was released in the dragon's breath. In the dragon-slaying legends, this power was absorbed into the hero who thereafter became an even mightier warrior.

Traditionally, dragons can be contacted and celebrated in various calls of the dragon, one of which is described below, to fill us with noble dragon strength and to access the stored knowledge within the collective wisdom of humankind, so we can generate our own treasures in life.

# Dragon Lore

Fafnir is the archetypal ruler of all earth and fire dragons in the eastern and western European traditions as well as in Scandinavia. However, the history of Fafnir is a strange one and the actual Fafnir was slain.

Norse myth records that the dwarf Regin persuaded his godson Sigurd (called Sigfried in Germany) to seek and kill Fafnir the dragon who had a fabulous hoard of treasure. However, Sigurd did not know that Fafnir was in fact the brother of Regin. In one version of the myth, Fafnir had been rewarded with a hoard of gold and gems by the gods. He was so afraid of losing it that he hid in a cave with it and over the years turned into dragon form because of his obsessive love for the gold.

Of course the whole dragon-slaying idea was actually a plot by Regin to seize the hoard for himself. Sigurd rode with Regin to find the dragon. At Regin's suggestion, they hid in a deep ditch and when Fafnir came to drink at a nearby pool, Sigurd stabbed his soft underbelly with his magical sword.

Regin cut out the heart of his brother and roasted it, but some of the hot fat dripped on Sigurd's finger. He licked the burn and immediately understood the language of the birds that told him Regin intended to kill him. Therefore Sigurd beheaded the dwarf and claimed the treasure and the wisdom of the birds.

In another interpretation, the dwarf Fafnir was guarding secret spiritual gold or wisdom, which he inherited from his father. This was the wisdom of the birds and the key to understanding their language. Understanding the language of the birds was a very secret and mystical art in the ancient world, for it was said that the birds could tell you all you needed to know about anything and even predict the future because they could listen to the words of the deities. It is said that Fafnir took on dragon form to keep the secret safe. It's hard to untangle the myth from the bias of the tellers.

Norse and European myths describe dragons in great detail as possessing all or some of the following: eagle's feet, batlike wings, the front legs of a lion, a reptile/dinosaur's head with a huge mouth and teeth from which smoke and fire pours, huge scales, the horns of an antelope, a soft under-belly, and a lizardlike tail that may begin close to the head.

Smaller fire drakes found in the myths of France and Germany do not have wings but are red with fiery breath. They are said to also be cave dwell-ers, where they live with their great hoards of the earth's riches.

According to Bulgarian dragon lore, the male dragon is the fire dragon and is a benign protector of humans and the crops in contrast to his watery, less well-disposed sister. Traditionally, Bulgarian dragons have three heads and wings. Dragon females are fiercely maternal, for it takes a thousand years for a dragon's egg to hatch and a further three thousand years for the young dragon to reach full maturity. Scandinavian and European eggs hatch sooner.

# Dragon Magick

Let's work with the most positive aspects of fire dragons. Working with fire dragons can transform our lives and bring a new, more securely based abun-dant world and creative life stage into being. Naturally, gold is the suggested tribute for attracting power, healing, and wealth in using dragon energies. However you can also use the crystal known as dragon's eggs, and if you work regularly with dragons it is well worth obtaining one of these from an online crystals store.[5] These are usually clear quartz, amethyst, or rose quartz in a pebble and are characterized by a polished glasslike window revealing the crystalline interior. These fabulous little treasures were once believed to be the eggs of dragons after the baby dragon had hatched.

## Finding Your Dragon-Magick Place

- Dragon caves are much wider, deeper, and darker than ordinary caves and may either be close to the sea (which dragons love) or in huge, rocky places, again near water.

- Alternatively find a site where "dragon" is part of the name of the place. Usually there is a dragon legend that goes along with the place.

- As with all magic, you can adapt if an ideal location isn't accessible. Go for a cave, a place where there are rocks with crevasses, or improvise any dark, enclosed place outdoors; even a tight circle of trees in your garden or a local park will work.

- You will need to take a dragon offering. This should be gold, for example a tiny gold earring. Alternatively substitute a golden-coloured coin.

- If you can get one, use a dragon egg to link you in with the power. If you don't have one, use a small, spherical clear quartz or round quartz crystal with lines and markings within the quartz.

- Gaze into the crystal or dragon egg as you sit in your chosen dragon place. Allow the occlusions and markings within the crystal to create images of your fire dragon that, because seen within this gentle crystal, are not at all intimidating.

- Now half-close your eyes but still hold your dragon egg or crystal. If the light is bright, you may *see* the swirling iridescent silver, purple, gold, green, and blue of the dragon outline shimmering ahead. Let the image enclose and energise you. Breathe slowly and regularly and allow the warm, shimmering colours to flow in and out of your own energy field, your aura.

- If you see nothing externally, close your eyes totally and allow the image to build up in your mind and superimpose it in your imagination on the scene.

- You might also see an image of a dragon within the cave your mind, but if you are lucky it might appear as an external, misty image.

- You may feel very warm as though close to a bonfire and see sparks or sunbeams dancing around in the air.

- When you are ready, close your eyes and gently push away with your hands, palms outwards and upright. Allow the energies to move away. You may sense them fading spontaneously as the dragon moves on.

- For this first encounter, do not ask for anything specific. The experience is enough and will help you to move with confidence and attract and spread the abundance you need.

- Be sure to take a bottle of water to drink afterward and splash on your hairline, brow, throat and wrists or palms to cool you down.

- Bury your tribute.

Now you are ready for a dragon ritual either in your dragon place or your outdoor fey area.

## A Dragon Spell for Gold

What "gold" do you need? Do you need health, a spurt of energy to see a task through, some money for your child's school trip, or perhaps the courage to take up the career you really want? Or do you need gold for a loved one who is struggling, healing for your sick pet, or to aid people in a war-torn area of the world? Do you want your book published or to win a talent contest?

### *You will need:*

- A flat, raised surface such as a rock to hold your spell materials.

- A small dish of dried tarragon herbs (called "the dragon herb"); you can also substitute parsley or sage. The herb should be placed directly in front of you and furthest away as you look ahead at your rock.

- A powdered dragon's blood incense stick or any spicy incense should be placed to the right side as you face the rock.

- A small, red candle directly in front of you and nearest to you.

- On the left side as you face the rock, place a bowl of water in which a carnelian, red or orange crystal, or red stone was soaked overnight.

- On the ground, place another larger bowl of water to the left and a bowl of soil to the right. These are placed on the ground to keep the spiritual energies cool and grounded.

- Place your dragon's egg, a white egg-shaped stone, your quartz crystal, an agate egg, or red flowers in the centre of the rock to symbolise your spell's focus.

## Timing:
Tuesday is a good dragon day; the day should be as bright as possible.

## The spell

- Though Southern Hemisphere directions are often different in magick, these dragon positions work well wherever you live in the world.

- Light the candle and say, "I call upon you, wondrous golden dragon, guardian of all treasures, not in greed, but in need. I kindle your flame and would welcome your shimmering presence."

- Light the incense from the candle and say, "I call upon you wondrous golden dragon, not in greed, but in need. I kindle your fragrance."

- With the smoke from the incense stick, draw the outline of a dragon as large as you can above, below, and all around yourself without moving your feet. Say, "I call upon you wondrous golden dragon that I may draw on your power not in greed, but in need. I kindle your image and your shimmering presence."

- Return the incense to its holder.

- Focus on the area around yourself and picture the shimmering, iridescent colours filling in the dragon outline and flowing within your own aura. You may start to feel warmth.

- Now you are going to try to extend your own connection with the dragon power.

- Pick up the dish of herbs and, as you walk on the ground surrounding your magical space, create a larger outline of your dragon with your footsteps or a large stick.

- Scatter tarragon around your imagined larger dragon image, saying, "So grows your fire, not to harm but to protect and bring abundance. I kindle your herbs with your shimmering presence."

- Replace the herb dish and continue to walk around your dragon with spiraling footsteps; if you wish, add drumming, chanting, or singing, calling to the power of the dragon to bring you the gold, not out of greed, but need.

- When you feel yourself filled with dragon power, blow out the candle, saying, "I seek gold and I pledge to share the rewards with those in need."

- Drop to the ground and sit motionless with your eyes closed and your arms outstretched like dragon wings and receive your gold. Wait until you feel the warmth receding and the dragon leaving.

- Speak your thanks and state how you will return the gift you now know is within you.

- Clear up quietly and pour the soil and then water it with the contents of the other bowl.

# Fire Spirits in the Wild,
# Will o' the Wisps, and Earth-Light Spirits

Nowhere is there more mystery or controversy than the manifestation of fire spirits as seemingly inexplicable lights in the sky that have been reported, for hundreds of years, in the same place. These are often called "earth lights," but in fact have far more in common with fire spirits and are close cousins of the mythical will o' the wisps.

In the Hessdalan Valley, about seventy miles southeast of Trondheim in Norway, white and yellow lights in the shapes of spheres, bullets, and inverted fir trees were first seen in 1981. These phenomena continued and in the summer of 1983; after hundreds of reports of earth lights from locals, Norwegian and Swedish UFO groups instigated Project Hessdalan. The area was continuously monitored for just over a month beginning on January 21, 1984. What is fascinating about this research is that the lights actually read the thoughts of the investigators and responded to them, suggesting the lights possess some form of objective consciousness.

## Defining the Phenomena

Lights often occur in areas of geological faults, earthquake zones, or ancient volcanic activity. It may be that just as earth spirits are energised by ley lines fire spirits are made visible by subterranean fire activity. Even more fascinating are the cases of well-researched Australian lights and American "northern lights" phenomena, there has often been an indigenous human tragedy or massacre in the area.

## Australian Lights / Fire Spirits

These lights in the sky are accepted as quite normal by indigenous people, such as aboriginal peoples of Kimberley in western Australia where there has been frequent activity over the years. They interpret the lights as manifestations of *djang* or supernatural energies.

Paul Devereux extensively researched the Kimberley lights in late 1995 with Erling Strand, a Norwegian researcher who was instrumental in the ground-breaking Norwegian Hessdalan project into light phenomena, and collected remarkably consistent accounts from members of the community.[6]

The most remarkable fire-spirit/earth light is the famous Min Min Lights, about sixty miles east of Boulia in southwest Queensland in Australia, once a thriving shearing centre. Bushmen first reported the lights as occurring around 1881 as a strange glow that grew to the size of a small watermelon and pursued them.[7]

Older aboriginals in the area consider that the Min Min Lights emanated from an old aboriginal burial ground and say they began after the destruction of the indigenous people was instigated.

Though it is just theory right now, and of course a number of lights do not neatly fit, the idea that fire spirits are being energised by underground fire sources in areas where tragedies may have occurred is a worthy line of study. In exploring this, we may better be able to understand these lights.

## The Brown Mountain Lights

Further support for our angry energised fire spirits comes from Jason Boone, an American psychic researcher. He told me about the lights of Brown Mountain in the foothills of the Blue Ridge Parkway just outside Morganton, North Carolina. According to official information, the lights are visible between sunset and sunrise, especially between 10:00 p.m. and 2:00 am and are most prevalent in September and October. Jason explained:

> *The lights have been seen since way back during the days of the Native Americans, first spoken of around 1200 [CE] when a battle was fought near the mountain between the Cherokee and Catawba Indians. The Cherokees tell that the lights are the Indian women still searching for their lost husbands and lovers.*
>
> *Scientists have stated that the cause could be sulphurous or other swamp gases that ignite once they reach the earth's surface. This isn't so because none of the gases are found in this area and there are no swamps in the region of Brown Mountain.*

> *Some people believe that the mountains are haunted by ghosts, faeries, and*
> *will o' the wisps. A few locals insist that the lights are linked with the sightings*
> *of what is known as "the woolly booger," a headless bear that has been sighted*
> *on the mountain on occasions.*

The lights vary in intensity and appearance from glowing balls of fire, skyrockets and whirling pinwheels of light.

## The Will o' the Wisps

In northern-European folklore, the well-documented floating fire spirits are called the "will o' the wisps" or "friar's lanthorn" (a flamelike phosphorescence). They were popularly regarded as a malevolent fire faeries who guard lost treasures. Will o' the wisps are said to elude all who attempt to follow them and lure many lost travelers to their end on marshes and bogs.

In Sweden, they are known as *lyktgubbe,* which means "the old man with the lamp." These flickering lights are usually seen in groups and float just above the ground. Others however say the luminous creatures actually help lost travelers. For this reason they are in some regions called "Jack o' Lanterns," giving their name to the Halloween turnip (now most commonly pumpkins) in the shape of a face that is placed in windows at Halloween to protect the household from harm. Yet other folklorists identify the lights as faery revels.

According to scientists from Isaac Newton onwards, the flamelike phosphorescence floating over marshy ground is due to the spontaneous combustion of decaying vegetable matter in the marsh. But research in 1980 by Dr. Alan Mills of England's Leicester University's Department of Geology was unable under laboratory conditions to reproduce a flame akin to will o' the wisps by the spontaneous combustion of methane, phosphene, or other hypothesised marshland gases. The researcher also could not discover any natural source of ignition. Moreover, these lights are frequently reported over mountain tops and on moorlands as well as over marshes.[8]

For example, in the Peak District in Derbyshire, a hilly area in central England, on a hill called Lantern Pike, is the home of an old mythical faery hag, Peggy-a-Lantern, who according to local folklore swings her lamp on the hilltop causing a phenomena that has also been witnessed by residents of the area for hundreds of years.

What is more, will o' the wisps have been known to respond to travelers, beckoning or calling them. It is the interaction between fire spirits, earth lights, and people that makes them especially remarkable.

## A Fire Spirit Ritual to Get Noticed Positively and for Fame and Fortune

### You will need:

An indoor or outdoor area lit by faery lights, the kind where the colours constantly change (string a set of outdoor faery lights on a tree using the outdoor socket normally used for lawn mowers). Alternatively, use two flashlights, one for each hand and a tube of gold glitter.

### Timing

Any Thursday (the day of power), Wednesday (the day of the performing arts), any night before career opportunity, or Tuesday for a huge leap forward. This should always take place after dark so that your light source is the only one (if necessary, draw curtains indoors).

### The spell

- Stand where there is no light and say, "I do not like the shadows of obscurity. I take my place in the light."
- Move to where the lights shine all over you or switch on the flashlights and swirl them over and all around your head about an arm's span away so that the light fills your aura energy field, the rainbow energies that surround us all. Say, "I welcome the chance to shine. Success be mine. You spirits of light and fire dance within me and make me radiant."
- Sprinkle glitter all around you, letting it fall on your clothes and in your hair. Say, "Let the light shine all around me, on me, and within

me. You spirits of light and fire dance within me and make me radiant. I seize this opportunity. You spirits of light and fire dance within me and make me radiant."

• Turn around very fast in the faery light or swirl your flashlights faster and faster until you become slightly dizzy. As you steady yourself, you will *see* the lights moving towards you and within you (a physiological phenomenon that you can use psychically). Say, "The light is within me. I cannot fail. I am pure light and fire."

• Switch off the lights or flashlights and in the darkness allow the momentary afterglow to fill you with radiance. The next morning, take the first steps to fame or make it known that you are interested in the position.

In the next chapter, we will explore the nature spirits of the waters.

---

Chapter 7 Sources

1. http://en.wikipedia.org/wiki/Salamander_(legendary_creature)

2. http://www.islamcan.com/jinn-stories.shtml

3. Burton, Richard, trans. *The Arabian Nights: Tales from a Thousand and One Nights.* New York: Modern Library Classics, 2004.

4. Heaney, Seamus. *Beowulf: A New Verse Translation.* New York: Norton, 2001.

5. www.charliesrockshop.com (shipped internationally from the UK a particularly high-quality and trustworthy supplier).

6. Devereux, Paul. *Earth Lights Revelation, UFOs, and Mystery Lightform Phenomena: The Earth's Secret Energy Force.* New York: Sterling Publishing, 1990.

7. http://www.castleofspirits.com/minmins.html

8. Will o' the wisp, http://www.devilspenny.com/2010/08/the-will-o%E2%80%99-the-wisp-more-than-just-swamp-gas/

# 8

## NATURE SPIRITS
## OF THE WATER

Water spirits are as varied as water itself—one moment calm, the next turbulent, always moving, inhabiting deep and still lakes, fast-flowing rivers, cascading waterfalls, and tumultuous oceans.

Though you may not get to know water essences or spirits individually, apart from one or two in places you regularly visit or those with local legends, you can easily connect with their powers because they are linked so strongly with human emotions.

### Water-Spirit Magical Associations

**Archetypal elemental spirit:** Undines, who originated in the Aegean Sea; they live in coral caves under the ocean, on the shores of lakes or banks of rivers or on marshlands in other lands. Undines shimmer with all the colours of water in sunlight and are so insubstantial they can rarely be seen with the physical eye, except as rainbows dancing on the waters.

**Water spirits ruler:** Niksa, Nicksa, Nixsa, or Neksa who rises from
the sea translucent, rainbow-coloured, riding a giant sea horse or in a
pearly or sea-green chariot pulled by white sea horses. Niksa has long
flowing hair, knotted with shells and a swirling cloak in all the colours
of the sea, edged with pearls. She loves pearls above all other gems.
Her voice may be soft and melodious like the mermaids she rules or
terrible as the stormy sea. She lives in deep coral caves far beneath the
sea. Niksa is attended by the oceanides, the beautiful sea-nymph daughters of Oceanus, Lord of the Sea.

**Favourite time of day:** sunset and twilight

**Favourite season:** autumn

**Energy:** passive and moving

**Character:** the integrator and peacemaker

**Elemental tool:** chalice

**Water-spirit ritual substance:** water

**Favourite colours:** blue or silver

**Psychic gifts they offer:** healing, telepathy, and scrying

**Polarity:** Goddess

**Water-spirit energy-raising:** rattles, prayer, and meditation

**Deities:** Moon and love deities, sea, sacred well and water gods and goddesses, goddesses of initiation and the mystery religions

**Archangel:** Gabriel Archangel of the Moon, clothed in silver or dark blue
with a mantle of stars and a crescent moon for his halo, a golden horn,
and white lily, alternatively with a lantern in his right hand and with a
mirror made of jasper in his left.

**Water-spirit crystals:** apatite, aquamarine, calcite, coral, enhydro quartz, fluorite, jade, moonstone, mother of pearl, opal, opal aura, pearl, selenite, and tourmaline

**Water-spirit animals and birds:** All fish, especially salmon, beavers, crabs, crocodiles and alligators, dolphins, ducks, frogs, herons, otters, platypus, sea horses, seals, starfish, swans and all water birds, whales

**Water-spirit fragrances:** apple blossom, apricot, coconut, eucalyptus, feverfew, heather, hyacinth, jasmine, lemon, lemon balm, lilac, lily, myrrh, orchid, passion flower, peach, strawberry, sweet pea, thyme, valerian, vanilla, and violet

**Ailments and body parts especially healed by water spirits:** Womb and genitals, hormones and glands, hands, all bodily fluids, tear ducts, emotions

**Sense:** sixth sense

**Positive qualities/strengths offered by water spirits:** ability to merge and interconnect with nature, beauty, compassion, empathy, fertility, forgiveness, inner harmony, gradual growth, harmonising with the cycles of the seasons, the moon and the life cycle, love, peacemaking, purity, sympathy for others, unconscious wisdom

**Less desirable qualities:** excesses in many areas of life, instability, lack of motivation, manipulation, possessiveness, and sentimentality

**Water-spirit places:** Aquariums, estuaries, flood plains, lakes, marshlands, oceans and the sea, pools and ponds, rivers and tidal rivers, sacred wells and springs, streams, waterfalls, water parks, and whirlpools

**Materials for attracting water spirits:** silver, copper, crystal spheres, dark and misty mirrors, fish in tanks or sea creature and dolphin images, inks, kelp (seaweed), milk, nets or webs of any kind, oils, reflections in water, saltwater, sea shells, scrying bowls, silver bells on cords, silver foil, steam, tides, water features, and wine

**Astrological signs:** Pisces, Cancer, and Scorpio

**Planets:** Neptune, the Moon, and Pluto

**Empowerment to call the power of the water spirits:** "May what is no longer needed in my life flow away on the ebb tide and love and peace return on the flow."

**Use water-spirit magick for:** astral travel; changing bad luck to good luck; friendship; healing using the powers of nature and especially from sacred water sources; love; peaceful or psychic dreams; purification rites; relationships; safe travel by sea; the mending of quarrels; to bring protection to those far away; and water, sea, and moon magic. It is also potent for cleansing sea, lake, and river pollution; campaigns for fresh water to parts of the world where there is none; fighting floods; world health initiatives; and care of whales, dolphins, seals, and all endangered sea creatures.

## Discovering the Spirits of the Seas

### Undines

These are the representative spirits of all waters, not just the sea, though they are primarily sea spirits.

Undines are small, beautiful water sprites that often resemble sea horses when in the ocean. Sometimes they ride on the waves and appear as pearly foam. They also dance around rock pools at low tide or in salt marshes. In marshes they may wear green glass beads.

Because they are the most insubstantial of the water spirits they are usually perceived (even by clairvoyants) only as distant rainbows on the waters, even on dark days, though children see them clearly.

Some Greek islanders claim kinship from the saltwater undines. Though undines are primarily spirits of the Aegean Sea, they are found in different forms in other lands, especially in warmer waters worldwide. They care for all the sea creatures, water plants, and coral.

Freshwater undines are even smaller and sleep beneath water lilies. They have wings, but unlike faeries that they resemble, they only live in plants and flowers close to water or near estuaries.

In some European folklore, undines are considered wandering spirits of lovelorn women whose tears salt the oceans.

### Undine Magick

Undines grant wishes of all kinds and bring spontaneity, love, joy, fertility, overcoming betrayal, and offering reconciliation in love because they themselves suffered loss. They bring blessings on babies, children, and families, family loyalty, and safe long-distance travel. They also enhance psychic powers.

## Nereides

They are the less-benign form of the undines and are the daughters of Doris, an Oceanid sea nymph and the sea god Nereus, the original Old Man of the Sea. They are originally descended from the oceanides, the 3,000 daughters of Oceanus, the ocean, and Tethhys the sea goddess.

Nereides are found throughout the Mediterranean regions of Greece and parts of eastern Europe, but especially love the Aegean ocean and the bays around Crete.[1] However, as with undines, you can work with their energies anywhere in warmer waters.

Though Pliny, the first-century Roman naturalist and philosopher, described the nereides as covered in scales, generally they are pictured as being beautiful with wonderful singing voices, shell headdresses, and riding hippocampi (horse-shaped dolphins). Each nereid rules over a body of water.

The nereides are said to drive mad or strike blind any man who perceives them under a full moon. They do not have souls and live twice as long as a tortoise. They envy human mothers their immortal souls and kidnap mortal infants, raising them in coral caves. Still, they can be benign, bless children, and protect sea travelers if given offerings. Thetis, the firstborn nereid, was the mother of the hero Achilles and is the spirit of calm seas.

They can venture on land wearing a white shawl, which if stolen gives the mortal who takes it power over them. In this way, they could be forced into marriage, but would escape, leaving husband and children once they regained the shawl. They also shape-shift as swans; in this form, their lovely but hypnotic voices may be heard, calling through the mist.

*Nereides Magick*

In their most benign aspects, the nereides bring freedom from pain, addiction, depression, and restrictions; provide protection for those traveling by sea or overseas; bring blessings on family life; lend power for reinventing oneself; and enhance musical gifts.

Smaller, faster-moving sea spirits like the undines and nereides are best for swift-moving matters or petitions, short-term blessings, and for hastening anything that is stagnant or slow. They are also useful in changing prevailing attitudes and situations to bring personal transformation in lifestyle and perspective.

## Merpeople

Human in appearance from the waist up, mermaids have long, golden hair and beautiful faces and fish- or porpoise-like body in place of the legs. Mermen are less attractive and benign and cause storms if annoyed or jealous of sailors who are attracted to their women.

Sailors have brought back tales of beautiful sea women with lovely voices, from all parts of the world and in all ages, telling how mermaids especially have saved drowning sailors and guided ships away from rocks.

Mermaids have, according to myth, married mortal men, usually through trickery on the part of the human who steals one of their possessions like their pearl mirror or comb as they sit sunning themselves on the rocks. This object binds them to dry land until the mermaid can retrieve it.

Mermaids live for three hundred years. However, in the most famous mermaid story of all time by Hans Christian Andersen it was the mermaid who was rejected by the mortal.[2] If you go to Copenhagen you will see the Little Mermaid statue in the harbour at Langelinie. It was erected in 1913 in memory of Andersen, Denmark's most famous writer, and has become a symbol of Denmark.

### Do Mermaids Actually Exist?

A strange story comes from Germany that suggests they may, though I have not been able to date it more precisely than the late 1800s. A man named Brauhard, who was a sailor, returned home to his native Lautenberg with a mermaid wife. He built her a huge tub of water in the house so she could still swim when she wanted. But local people became very angry and the mermaid was mysteriously poisoned. Brauhard was grief-stricken, for he loved his beautiful mermaid so much. According to folklore he used the money given by her mer father to help the local poor. It is told that this wealth started the Brauhard Fund, which even today exists for the benefit of local people in need. Of course, Brauhard could have acquired the wealth by trading, but many do believe the story.[3]

### Merpeople Magick

Mermen and especially mermaids bring love and fertility, find what is lost, provide safety in travel, improve likelihood of wishes coming true, bring good luck (especially in gaining unexpected treasures), enhance the developing of artistic and musical talents, allow the overcoming of jealousy or possessiveness in love, and fulfil seemingly impossible dreams.

## Selkies

These seal men and women live around the shores of Scotland, Ireland, and North America and as far north as southern Scandinavia.

Selkies are great shape-shifters. They often assume mortal form on land and sometimes marry a human husband or wife, but eventually return to their own world. Seal men would come ashore, take off their sealskins and settle in a house with a wife and have a child. Of course they were excellent fishermen, especially by night when they would put on their sealskins and dive into the water. But they would stay with their wives for only a year and a day and after that would return to the sea.

If their wives needed them, the women would set a candle in a sea-facing window or take a lantern down to the shore and call their loves who would return for a while.

Selkie women are said to be less powerful. Like mermaids, they could be held against their will if the mortal husband locked away or hid the seal-skin without which they could not return to the waters. The following is a typical story from the Scottish Hebrides.[4]

A fisherman of the McCodrum clan saw seven beautiful selkie sisters dancing on the shore. Nearby on rocks were seven sealskins. By stealing one of the skins he was able to capture a selkie who lived with him in her mortal form. They had one or two children, depending on the version. As years went by, she lost her beauty. Her skin flaked and she became so exhausted she could hardly move. So she searched for her sealskin, for she knew only by return-ing to the water could she survive. At last the selkie discovered her sealskin, locked in a cupboard, wrapped herself in it and returned to the waves.

In some versions of the myth, her only son finds the skin, restores it to his mother and dives into the waves with her and meets his grandfather. Though he returns to live with his father, the boy often sits on the rocks and his mother sings to him.

The clan, it is said, was thereafter called McCodrum of the Seals and they are gifted with the second sight of the faery people and reputed to be as at home on the water as on land.

*Selkie Magick*

Use selkie magick for healing and the restoration of health and energy, establishing or regaining your unique identity, overcoming relationship difficulties and gentle partings, success in dance and sports (particularly those related to water), for family loyalty, and reuniting lost or estranged family members.

Mermaids and selkies can be invoked for longer-term wishes, commitments, and plans and for overcoming major obstacles to allow life and love to flow again.

## Working with the Changing Moods of the Sea Spirits

Many sea spirits or sprites are not as clearly identifiable as those I have described and are the guardians of the specific shores you visit.

The sea has her moods like the weather, as well as ebbs and flows of high, low, and slack tides. These directly reflect and are reflected in moods of the sea people. A tide table will identify the relevant tide you need.

- Ingoing or outgoing, a calm sea is ideal for harmony and peace, making wishes, stability, improving finances or career, finding and maintaining love and happiness, righting family matters, protecting children and pets, safe travel, and happy holidays.

- In contrast, a stormy sea brings changes and movement, justice, a sudden rush of confidence, determination, courage to take a stand against bullies, and overcoming obstacles.

- Incoming tides restore or bring good luck, love, fertility, travel, and prosperity.

- Use the slack tide that may last an hour or more, between high and low tides as they prepare to turn, with no real current flow, to gently launch desires, especially for longer-term results into the still water (easiest around a harbour) to be carried when the sea is ready, either in or out.

• Slack tides balance emotions, people, or priorities that are pulling you in opposite directions and to your home and life after instability.

• The ebb tide or outgoing tide washes away ill health, finance or career problems, a destructive relationship, or bad luck, and reduces negativity, spite, and malice.

• The moon also affects the sea and the sea spirits. The week after the new moon and the week of the full moon have particularly strong and extreme tides. The night of the full moon or those immediately before and after are superb for paddling out to sea, sailing, and casting spells or dropping tributes into deep moonlight rock pools.

## Talking with the Sea Spirits

• Visit a particular shore regularly if possible, during different times, seasons, and weathers to tune in to the local sea spirits and learn legends and names.

• If you live far from the ocean or a tidal river, holidays are ideal for encountering different indigenous sea beings. Though Greece is traditionally home of many sea spirits, Florida, California, and the gentler beaches of Australia have similar energies. Cold Atlantic seas have fiercer, braver energies, but do not be deterred as the spirits have dynamic, tough energies.

• Paddling, swimming, sailing, making sand castles on the shore, or collecting shells and fossils give you a physical connection with the wave rhythm and sounds.

• Listen to the voices of the spirits in the sound of the waves. They will answer questions you ask out loud into the sea breeze.

• Visualise a sea creature of your own for each of the sea stages, tides, and moods or picture the same spirit in different garments and

movements. You may see many sprites or one more majestic sea
mother guardian.

• Children love throwing shells and stones into the waves or making
circles on the sand and writing their names or wishes in the circle
for the sea to cover and carry to fruition. This can also be practised
by adults.

• Write, draw, and photograph the changing sea. Using a computer,
you can turn photographs into paintings, and suddenly you see a
wave surge emerges as the image of a sea being on your screen.

## Seeking the Blessings of the Sea Spirits

• Sea spirits should not be taken for granted as wish granters. There are
times when you sense it is right to seek a blessing, when to make an
offering, or when to just sit quietly and listen to the wise words of
the waves.

• Once you have made your connection with the prevailing sea mood
and tide, picture any special kind of sea spirit or mermaid with whom
you desire to work or allow the image and perhaps voice of the local
sea sprite to come into your mind if you have not already met the sea
spirit of the local shore.

• Let the spray blow over you or paddle out a little way, to the seventh
or ninth waves which are traditionally associated with sea spirits.

• Decide in advance what you are offering the sea in return for the
blessings you seek. A tiny pearl, a small aquamarine, some white
flowers, or a small piece of fruit. These are especially appropriate.
Maybe you need more than one offering if your request is complex
or urgent.

• Find a large piece of driftwood as an offerings boat.

- Next, find something cast up on the shore that belongs to the sea; a beautiful shell; a small piece of seaweed; a naturally occurring shore crystal such as amber, jet, or quartz; or a feather from a sea bird. Alternatively, you could use a small piece of driftwood and with a knife make a sea-spirit figure from it.

- Set your offering and the treasure belonging to the sea on your driftwood boat. If you are working after twilight, balance a small pre-lit, flat beeswax candle or environmentally friendly tea light on the wood.

- Paddle out or wait for the seventh or ninth wave to hit shore and carefully launch your offerings boat.

- Ebb tides are best for launching boats, but if the tide is incoming, cast the offerings directly on to the waves.

- As you do so, name the sea spirit or spirits aloud. If you do not have a name, say, "Kind spirit of the sea," and picture a sea spirit rising from the sea.

- If working with merpeople or selkies, you can set your offerings boat on rocks that will be covered by the tide as it comes in.

- Greet the sea spirits and say, "I return what is your treasure back to you and I offer my treasure as token of my thanks and in blessings."

- At this point if the energies feel right say, "I would ask your help to bring [name of desired person or thing]."

- If you can do something to help the sea and those who live by fishing or as sailors; perhaps make a small donation if you can afford it to the local sea rescue service or a fisherman's charity.

- Ask permission to take a small piece of seaweed (kelp) home and put it in a jar covered with whisky; place the jar on a window ledge to attract prosperity and good fortune.

## A Shell Wish Spell for Restoring What Is Lost

This is a very effective spell for calling a lover from overseas whether apart because of career or estrangement; for any reconciliation in love with a partner or for family unity; also for the restoration of what is owed or rightfully yours and for regaining money after a loss.

There are many spells where a symbol is enclosed in two halves of a shell tied together or a single half shell to carry your wishes on the tide. This spell utilises a single, round half shell.

### *You will need:*

An open half shell that is hollow, preferably found on the shore before the spell. Take one with you in case you cannot find one.

A very small, perfectly round, white stone, also preferably found on the shore before the spell.

A small piece of gold (such as an earring or coin) or a tiny sea crystal like aquamarine, ocean or orbicular jasper, or coral as your offering.

### *Timings:*

Just before high tide. You can use any flowing water if you cannot go to the shore, but call the sea spirits and they will hear no matter how far away; they exist on the astral or spirit plane that is without boundaries. Put just a tiny taste of salt on your tongue if you are casting your spell in non tidal waters. If the need is urgent, use a large glass bowl of water to which you have added three pinches of salt and swirled the bowl around nine times in each direction.

## The spell:

- Hold the stone in your cupped hands and softly speak your wish for what must be restored and the time scale you desire and ask the spirits of the sea to aid your endeavour and return what or whom you have lost if it is right to be.

- Put the stone in the shell with your offering. Holding the shell in cupped hands, repeat your request, adding, "Spirits of the ocean, fey of the sea, I return what is yours, return mine to me."

- Leave the stone and your offering in the shell just below the high tide line so the sea will cover it before the tide turns. Make the request again, once more adding, "Spirits of the ocean, fey of the sea, I return what is yours, return mine to me."

- If you prefer, launch it on an ebb tide.

- Turn away in both cases and do not look back.

## The Water Sprites of the Fresh Waters

The term *water sprite* is also applied to smaller, sometimes shape-shifting fresh water spirits. Water sprites are the spirits of waterfalls, rivers, and lakes and are numerous throughout the world. Some of these nature essences are welcoming to humans, but others can be unpredictable or dangerous, reflecting the hazards of the deep or fast-flowing waters that they rule. Parents in different lands may in times past exaggerated the ugly frightening aspects of water spirits of dangerous places to warn off their children and many of these frightening creatures acquired names and legends.

### Water Nymphs or Naiads

Naiads are specifically nymphs of rivers, springs, and fountains who live in caves near or in water or under the surface of rivers, though the term is frequently used as a general term for all water nymphs.[5]

Naiads, according to Greek legend, were beings spiritually placed between the gods and mortals. They were the daughters of the river gods who feasted on ambrosia, a divine honey. They are believed to endow water with healing properties and so many floral offerings have been made to them at river crossings or sources of rivers.

Streams, springs, and rivers everywhere have similar water spirits who care for animals and the purity of the water source. Oreads are the mountain spring dwellers. Both kinds of nymph die if the water source dries up.

Even benign water spirits can be ambivalent; research any local legends to find out any prohibitions they may impose on communication. For example, while those mortals born on a Saturday are permitted to watch naiads dancing, it is considered dangerous for others to approach them especially in full moonlight (their favourite time for revels).

## Waterfall Spirits

### Fossegrim

Fossegrim are quicksilver Norwegian and Swedish waterfall sprites, which are most usually seen in the foam in pools, at the base of waterfalls or in the waterfall pool. They also protect fjords and large inlets. They are invariably kind and guard those who come near the waterfall, especially animals and children.[6]

Fossegrim are described as beautiful blond boys or maidens whose feet disappear in the foam. They gently cleanse any doubts, fears, or pointless situations and remove pain and sickness. Should you be able to safely access the area behind a small waterfall, you may actually see fossegrim or similar water spirits in the foam, wherever you are in the world. Throw small crystals into the waterfall and ask the Fossegrim for the release you seek.

### Fossegrim Music

Famed for their mesmeric voices and melodies that merge with the sounds of the waterfall, fossegrim are exquisite harpists and according to myth have taught many famous human harpists throughout time.

At twilight, go to connect with these gentle harmonies and healing songs that will bring good luck, harmony, joy, love both for a significant other and self-love, better health, musical abilities, or happiness to those who hear them.

After any Fossegrim encounter, you will not be able to recall their songs, except in sleep when you may dream of floating on a boat along a river; in the morning, however, you will feel healed of stress and ready to make real progress in the waking world.

## Working with Friendly Water Sprites

Water sprites of all kinds are often seen as ripples within flowing water or rising as rainbow bubbles, especially at dusk and dawn in spring and autumn. Natural thermal pools (such as Mataranka thermal pools, the Bitter and Rainbow Springs south of Katherine in the Northern Territory of Australia, or the healing and fertility hot springs at Alama de Granada in southern Spain) are also potent water-spirit sites.

If you splash the sparkling water on you or, where possible, paddle, float, swim, or sail, you will discover that everything in your life begins to flow quite naturally before long. What you need flows in and what you no longer want flows away. Children who play supervised in or near natural bodies of fresh water as opposed to chlorinated swimming pools become joyful and far less hyperactive and irritable.

- Get yourself into rhythm with your chosen water, focusing on a waterfall or flowing water source or look deep into a lake or pool when light is rippling on the surface and let your personal boundaries relax, like taking off a tight work suit and shoes that pinch.

- Touch the water and then slowly withdraw your hand so the water droplets shimmer off your skin.

- Do this several times slowly and rhythmically so that you feel the water and the nature of the spirit, sparkling and bubbly, slow and warm or ice-cold even in summer.

- Listen to the sound of the water and follow the patterns of light. Before long, you will sense that the water is alive and that its energy vibrations and yours are moving in tune.

- Let a water-sprite image form in your mind and then visualise it as part of the water. Don't force the connection, but let the connection and image come as you splash around with your hand. Before long, you will link with the moods and feelings of the water spirit.

- Afterward, find out if there are any local water-sprite legends. You usually discover that your own impressions were remarkably similar to those beings portrayed in the legends.

- Try different kinds of fresh water; dive, wade in and swim, or take a small kayak or canoe so you are close to the physical water. Row, paddle, or swim rhythmically to pick up the sprite movement. If you dive down and splash up, you may momentarily see your sprite in front of you as you brush water droplets from your eyes. If not, splash your face with water and blink.

- Experience an accessible water place in rain so water cascades from above and below (beware of lightning, however). White-water rafting tends to be too intense if you are new to water spirit work, but once you are connected with spirit water flow some very exciting spirits will rise and fall with you.

- Visit your favourite water places in different weathers and seasons and get in tune with the changing moods of the water sprite and their excitement before a rain storm.

- Go in snow and break the ice on a pool or lake and see the sprites sparkle. In time, one or two sprites may become favourites and you can visit their water to carry out simple rituals or just sit beside it, looking through half-closed eyes to restore harmony with the world.

- Places with wildlife or water fowl will always be especially vibrant with water sprites.

- When abroad, visit sacred springs, lakes, and rivers and learn the history and legends of their spirits.

- In your fey journal, record the different moods of still and flowing water spirits—those who inhabit a gentle stream; a small, still pool; or a cascading waterfall; seen in misty sunlight, moonlight, or in wind.

## Lake Spirits

Every lake has its guardian whose name is often a variation of the lake name itself.

Some lakes in Christian times were given the title of Holy Lake, in memory of the attempts by local monks or priests to banish the lake spirits who were unfairly blamed for drowning and the lack of fish. According to local legend, Holy Lake near the village of Neuhoff, Germany, not far from the Elbe River in the district of Wolmirstedt, was the home of Brother Nixel, a not-so-friendly water spirit common in Germany. Burkhard, the Archbishop of Magdeburg between 1295 and 1304 CE, blessed the lake and proclaimed he had cast out all the heathen spirits (he added a few banished ghosts for good measure). Of course, the local people continued to offer tributes to the water sprites and the clergy blamed the inevitable occasional drowning on human sin.

### The Lady of the Lake

Sometimes there may be a single lake lady, sometimes served by eight water women of slightly lesser rank.

The Lady of the Lake is invariably dressed in white. She walks upon the water on misty days and lives in a glass or crystal palace beneath the lake. Most famous is the glass palace of Viviane, the French Lady of the Lake who became the lover of Merlin the magician who advised King Arthur. According to myth, Merlin built her a palace of glass beneath a lake in the forest of Broceliande near Rennes in Brittany and taught her all he knew of magic. You can see the palace beneath the lake if you gaze into the still waters on a sunlit day, for the lake is like glass. (There is a King Arthur Museum nearby.[7])

## Ladies of the Lake

In Wales, there are many lake women who live with their fathers and brothers beneath the deep Welsh lakes set among the mountains. The most famous are the *gwragedd annwyn,* golden-haired female Welsh water faeries, living in palaces beneath the lakes of the Black Mountains. They are the same size as humans and are kind to children, those without money, and to mothers. These lake maidens have on occasions taken human husbands, though they rarely stay with them. Some local families living close to the lake still claim lake women heritage. One may act as a queen.

The most famous is the Lady of the Lake of Llyn y Fan Fach. She is reputedly the faery ancestor of an unbroken line of Welsh healers and physicians, and unusually, this faery legend can be dated. Around 1230 CE, records tell that a young farmer saw three beautiful women dancing on the shore.

The loveliest lake maiden agreed to be his wife, and her father, the king of faery, came from under the lake to bring a dowry of faery cattle. However, he imposed a number of conditions on his daughter. One was that she should never be touched with iron, another that she should not be made to go to church, and if her husband struck her three times she and her dowry would return to the lake.

The couple had three sons, but the farmer broke his bargain, hit her and forced her to go to church, so she and her cattle returned to the lake. However she did come back to teach her sons knowledge of herbs and healing. They became the Physicians of Myddfai, healers to the Welsh kings. When they died, they left a medical treatise, copies of which exist today in Cardiff Castle museum.[8] The small, sturdy, brown cattle that thrive in the mountainous landscape of Wales are said to be descended from faery cattle, given as dowry with the lake women.

The Tylwyth Teg is the more generalised name for lake women in different parts of Wales. Their name means the "fair family" and they are also known as Bendith y Mamau, "Mothers' Blessing."

### Lake Lady Rituals

All over the world, lakes have been found with offerings of gold, metal cups, bronze drinking horns, coins, and statues of water deities, some dating back thousands of years. Lake ladies expect offerings that are emotionally precious to you, whether a small piece of gold jewelry, a water crystal such as fluorite, a tiny crystal angel, a soapstone animal, or a wooden statue.

- Early morning is good for lake-lady rituals for new beginnings, new love, the growth of money or health, happiness at home, to bring love to fruition, commitment, fidelity, to conceive a child, or healing for an animal or place.

- Twilight is good for letting go of anything, as the sun sets over the water.

- Darkness sheds pain, fear, depression, and addiction and brings acceptance of what cannot be changed.

- Before you begin, spend time connecting with the lake guardian, speaking in your mind or softly aloud those thoughts, worries, and dreams you might tell your mother or best friend, or maybe which are too private to share even with them.

- When you are ready, pick up your tribute.

- Cast your tribute into the lake from the waterside.

- You can paddle or swim out with the tribute. In the winter, wade out in waterproof boots.

- Alternatively, sail or row, taking your tribute to the centre of the lake and let it go.

• Hold the tribute in cupped hands and weave a gentle, flowing wish; for example, "Lady of the still waters, Lady of the Lake, let [fertility/ love/commitment/healing/reconciliation] flow into my life and [unhappiness/abuse/loneliness/pain] flow from me, lady of the still waters, Lady of the Lake." Cast your tribute into the water and say, "I make my gift to you with blessings, asking yours, fair mother of blessing."

• Stand or sit silently and watch the tribute float, create ripples, or sink straight away.

• Picture or physically see a soft, white hand reaching up to take the offering. You may notice ripples or sunlight sparkling around the place on which you focus.

• Thank the guardian; when you are ready, continue with your day's fun activities.

## Less Amiable Water Spirits

In deep, dark pools or treacherous stretches of river, myth tells us that malevolent spirits were believed to reside. It was dangerous to bathe in these places, not only because of the malicious spirit, but in practical terms because of hidden currents or sudden depth change.

Though some bad-tempered water spirits were given a generic name like *nokken* in Sweden or *nixes* in Germany, others developed individual personalities and legends of their origin.

In northern England lives Jenny Greenteeth.[9] Her hair is said to be the green plants floating on water. She was originally associated with the Ribble River in Lancashire, specifically the stepping stones near Brungerley. Here every seven years she was said to snatch a child and drag her under the water, a warning to be careful of the fast-flowing river and the slippery stones.

Jenny's fame spread, and I have even found an account of Jenny on the Isle of Wight off the south coast of England at a theme park called Blackgang

Chine (the park is set on a ley line). Here was a beautiful green-clad water maiden who would seduce unwary young men and then turn into a hideous hag and drag them to her watery home, as well as drowning children. In more suspicious times, the fey were unfairly blamed for disappearances, drowning, and abductions that were either accidents or human malice.

If you feel unusually negative vibes when near water, especially if your children are playing and you feel suddenly anxious though you have taken every precaution, you may be receiving a warning that all is not well. There may be unusual water conditions or weather approaching; perhaps a heavy rain has caused flooding, a drought has cast up rocks, or the water swell for sailing may suddenly deteriorate. Do not panic or leave immediately, but listen to the message or images that come into your mind from the spirit of the place and remain alert. If the place is unfamiliar, check with locals about quicksand or hidden currents.

## Indigenous Fierce Water Creatures

In lands with strong indigenous cultures, such as Native American or Australian aboriginal cultures, there are often inherited legends of fearsome water beings from the original inhabitants of the land. From my own research, these scary creatures are most prevalent where powerful earth energies can be felt at the intersection of leys or at natural vortex points.

For example, the bokwus is a malevolent Native American male spirit found near rushing water, especially in the Pacific Northwest of the United States. His fierce, war-painted face may be glimpsed peering behind trees as he seeks to drown and capture their souls of unwary fishermen or hunters.

### The Australian Bunyip

Aboriginals speak of fearsome booming bunyip monsters that inhabit swamps and waterholes. While I was traveling through Queensland with my friend Konnie, we encountered a bunyip statue larger than a human ten-minute drive from the peaceful town of Mulgidie. Over the years, tales have emerged from aboriginal people and drovers of bubbling, churning water in legendary bun-yip holes and cattle disappearing in the depths as they drank.

Aboriginal elders say the bunyip waterhole is connected by vast under-ground caverns passing the Tellebang Mountain that stretch as far as the Ban Ban Springs. These springs are a sacred site to the aboriginals, associated with the dreamtime, the ever-present time of creation, marking where the creat-ing Rainbow Serpent began his journey making waterholes and forming the landscape. He still protects the site. The waters are warm and though by the side of the main Burnett highway the Ban Ban springs are misty and mystical.

Accounts of this fearsome water spirit appear in indigenous accounts as well as in the 1850s in settler accounts. Descriptions from nineteenth-century newspaper reports include a doglike face, dark fur, a horselike tail, flippers, walrus-type tusks or horns, and even a duck bill. The Challicum bunyip, an outline image of a bunyip carved by Aboriginal people into the bank of Fiery Creek near Ararat, Victoria, was first recorded by the *Australasian* newspaper in 1851. A large number of bunyip sightings occurred between the 1840s and 1850s, particularly in the southeastern colonies of Victoria, New South Wales, and South Australia, as European colonization continued.[10]

The bunyip's apparent usual method of killing its prey is by hugging it to death. However bunyips are not all bad news; they have also been said to guide fishermen to good spots and protect them from dangerous swamp creatures.

## Bringing the Water Spirits into Our Homes

A water-spirit place can be set up anywhere in your home. Its spreading ener-gies will benefit family and visitors alike and ensure abundance, peace, health, and positive emotions flow freely through your home. Centre it around a small water feature or a tank of goldfish. In Feng Shui, the water area is centred in the north of your home or the north of a room in which you relax.

Enclose the space with green trailing plants; tiny indoor lemon trees; and water crystals such as orbicular or ocean jasper, green jasper, pearls, green and purple fluorite, jade, and aquamarine.

Add water symbols such as a lucky Chinese toad with a coin in its mouth or a turtle to encourage prosperity, shells, and natural driftwood sculptures formed by the sea.

Have a glass bowl filled with water for offerings of tiny water crystals (a broken pearl necklace is ideal) you drop in when you or a family member ask for a particular blessing.

When you next visit a local water place, take offerings along in a little waterproof bag (you can fish them out with a net) and offer them to the local spirits.

In the next chapter, we will look at the fiercer spirits of nature.

---

## Chapter 8 Sources

1. http://www.theoi.com/Pontios/Nereides.html

2. Andersen, Hans C. *The Little Mermaid*. New York: Minedition, 2004.

3. Eason, Cassandra. *Fabulous Creatures, Mythical Monsters, and Animal Power Symbols: A Handbook*. Santa Barbara, CA: Greenwood Press, 2007.

4. http://www.orkneyjar.com/folklore/selkiefolk/

5. http://www.pantheon.org/articles/n/naiads.html

6. Whyte, Saga. *Why the Naiads Dance*. Helsinge, Denmark: Whyte Tracks, 2010.

7. http://www.francemonthly.com/n/0106/index.php#article5

8. http://www.bbc.co.uk/blogs/waleshistory/2011/08/physicians_of_myddfai.html

9. http://en.wikipedia.org/wiki/Jenny_Greenteeth

10. http://www.ourpacificocean.com/australia_bunyips _mythology/index1.htm

# 9

~~~

# THE FIERCE CREATURES

As I have described in accounts in earlier chapters, fey creatures, depending on their mood, can be not only ambivalent toward humans, but occasionally malevolent.

If any area has a nasty energy, if grass does not grow, or there are no birds, be wary of using it as these are signs of the presence of more negative nature spirits. Such areas may have a name with the words "devil" or "demon." The little demons described in mediaeval religious literature are remarkably like goblins which I describe later in the chapter.

## Negative-Spirit Places

Jason Boone, the US researcher I mentioned in chapter 7 on fire spirits, described such an area called the Devil's Tramping Ground near Siler City in North Carolina. The Devil's Stamping Ground is a forty-foot circle of land in the middle of woodland on which only the sparsest of grass will grow. Around it is a circular path along which nothing at all will grow and anything dropped on the path disappears. Around the path, the devil is said to stamp in endless circles, thus rendering the land barren. People who camp near the Devil's Stamping Ground complain of strange noises and voices in the night and generally move on quickly.

Such spots are places where subterranean earth energies are soured or blocked, which can be caused by some human tragedy or evil on the land which attracts nature spirits intent on mischief. Another legend tells that the circle was once used for secret Native American ceremonies and the ground was cursed when the indigenous population were forced to leave and their noble spirits went with them, leaving less benign creatures to move in.

## Scary Places and Scary Faeries

Scary places have scary faeries, and this seems true in similar terrains across the globe. Imagine being lost in a dense jungle or deep forest. There is a sound in the undergrowth, mocking laughter. We scream. Who is it? It depends on where you are lost. The powerful Brazilian hobgoblin *curupira* spirit who is known as the lord of the jungle is described with red shaggy hair or as bald with huge ears. He has red eyes, double-jointed swollen knees, and cloven feet turned back to front to fool people who try to escape by looking at his footprints, as he can move in all directions. He wears calabashes or colourful gourds around his neck and on his legs. He has a wild cry, and sometimes rides a wild pig. He is not all bad, however; he protects tortoises from hunters, and in return for tobacco, finds lost cattle and only harms hunters who wound animals and do not go for a clean kill.

The *Dama Dagenda*, jungle spirits of Papua New Guinea, resent human intrusion into their home and not only refuse to guide or aid hunters who encounter them but can wound them with skin sores or lesions. The only way to escape is to speak in gibberish—that will fascinate them into trying to understand what the humans are saying. Another fierce forest spirit is the tiny wizened Papua New Guinea *kiliakai*, blamed for stealing mortal babies, pigs, and shooting small arrows causing malaria at mortals who dare to enter their territory. Small children wandering from a village becoming lost and killed by wild animals and jungleborne diseases such as malaria have long been blamed on nature spirits, so there is a huge crossover between what is fey malevolence and humans using them as a scapegoat in much the same way they have witches.

Across the world in the geographically unconnected region of dense Finland forests is the equally terrifying, often-female forest spirit, *Ajatar, Aiatar, Ajattaro*, or *Ajattarais*, called the "devil of the woods" or the "mother of the devil." She is also seen in the form of a female dragon or serpent and brings illness to all who look at her, spreads diseases, and is said to suckle snakes. She is perhaps a Christian reaction against an older mother goddess worship, for the pagan mother goddess was associated with snakes and later dragons.

## Goblins

Goblins are small, strong, and ugly, covered in black hair with eyes like glowing coals. They are spiteful creatures of the night and shun daylight; they roam in bands, terrifying and harassing travelers and children. Goblins are as unfriendly to other earth spirits as they are to humans, entrapping other faery folk, forcing them to work as slaves in their mines. Often regarded as the antithesis of the elves in Tolkien's *The Hobbit*, the goblin king captured and enslaved the dwarves and Bilbo for a time in the mines of Misty Mountains (see the suggested reading section, for Tolkien is a treasure store of fey wisdom).

Goblins are great shape-shifters, and turn into wild animals, bats, or owls. Goblins are also associated with the darker side of Halloween, their special festival when they roam unchecked over the earth. Though they are of Germanic and Scandinavian origin, goblins, like their larger cousins the Orcs, have been reported worldwide

## Orcs

Orcs can be bigger than a human male. They have leathery skins, a snout like a pig instead of a nose and tusks, and like goblins give off a sulphurous or rancid odour. Orcs are notorious in folklore for capturing other faery people and forcing them to work as slaves in their mines, in much the same way goblins do. They are the bullies of the spirit world and are especially attracted to bullying and intimidating young men in their twenties. Here are two case studies out of a number I have collected over the years.

Jason, the researcher who described the Devil's Stomping Ground, encountered his orc in North Carolina. He was in the Brown Mountains late in the evening after losing some friends on an overnight trek. Because he was an experienced walker he wasn't worried about finding his way back. It was getting dark and Jason entered a wooded area on the lower slopes. Ahead of him in the darkness he could see a black figure with eyes like burning coals that lunged at him with long, clawlike hands.

Jason fled, petrified because he had been brought up to believe in the devil and so he believed it was Satan himself pursuing him. Jason could smell sulphur, of course a sign of orcs and goblins. The creature pursued him and Jason was covered in scratches from where he had tripped until at last he saw the campsite where his friends were. He had a large, jagged scratch on his back where he had felt the creature clawing him.

The burning coal-like gleaming eyes and the blackness often described in demonic encounters through the ages are characteristics shared by orcs and goblins.

The second story is about Pehr; he was in his twenties and was staying in his grandmother's summer hut on the Sweden–Finland border, many miles from the nearest building. Twice when he was walking home at night through the forests after trekking he was chased by what he described as a life-sized hideous black form with glowing coal-like eyes. On both occasions, he could hear it breathing outside the hut. But there was a cross on the wall as Pehr's grandmother was very religious, and so the creature did not enter.

Many mediaeval monks in Europe and Scandinavia thought they were being tormented by the devil, who was more likely a nasty tempered orc or goblin. Monasteries were frequently built on ley energy lines, because most monks, such as the Benedictines, knew all about them. Earth power attracts nature spirits, both good and bad.

# How to Create Enchantments
# to Banish Our Inner Goblins

Magically, orcs and goblins represent our darkest fears that we hide deep within us. Occasionally, they come bursting out, overwhelming us, causing us to perhaps panic in an elevator. We may binge eat and ruin a healthy eating plan, exercise obsessively to the detriment of our health, or break a self-imposed smoking detox because of sudden stress. These are the goblins that enslave us and encourage us to impose limitations on our life or press the self-destruct button.

I would suggest you begin with relatively small inner goblins, just two or three, so you get used to handling them, as it is better to take matters a day and a step at a time when it comes to confronting fears.

Create a mantra or empowerment you can repeat over and over at times when those self-destructive urges hold us in their sway. One example might be, "Light is stronger than darkness and I am stronger than you, dark goblins. Be gone with your foul-smelling breath and your bullying. I am free."

## Overcoming the Goblins and Orcs

In time as you become more confident you can work with more fearsome orcs who may symbolise traumatic events from childhood or your past that you perhaps have buried, but which may surface unexpectedly and make it hard to love or trust. Be gentle with yourself and if you feel panicky say your mantra and then spend time walking or doing a physical activity, preferably outdoors. This is also an excellent ritual to do on behalf of a child or teenager who is being bullied or influenced to behave destructively, and can aid in defeating injustice.

### *You will need:*

- A red candle and a bowl of water.

- A small smudge stick in sagebrush or cedar or a large, firm incense stick in any tree fragrance.

- Garlic granules, the kind you use for cooking. These smell foul when burned, so keep all the windows open if working indoors and light rose or lavender incense or oil afterward. Garlic is especially effective against these creatures of the night.

### Timing:

Tuesday, but work just before sunset before the goblins and orcs fully emerge.

### The ritual:

- Whether you are indoors or out, set a small table with the items on it and stand facing whatever is the approximate north in front of the table.

- Hold the unlit candle in your nondominant hand; using the index finger of your dominant hand, invisibly trace all over the candle the words, *Goblins/orcs of* [your fear or problem], *be gone back to your dark places and leave me free.*

- Light the candle; this will release the power of light to overcome fears or dark thoughts. Repeat, *Goblins/orcs of* [your fear or problem], *be gone back to your dark places and leave me free.*

- Now light the incense or smudge. Draw a large circle around yourself, an extended arm span all around you and the table using the lighted incense or smudge like a smoke pen. Turn around to face the four directions, either clockwise in the Northern Hemisphere or counterclockwise in the Southern Hemisphere, until you have made a complete circle. The smoke circle of protection will extend even farther outward, but a tight circle is good to keep the goblins or orcs out. Repeat the chant until you have completed the circle.

- Return the smudge to its place.

- Drop a few granules of garlic into the candle flame and say, "Goblins of fear, dark creatures of temptation, light is stronger than darkness and I am stronger than you. Be gone with your foul-smelling breath and your bullying. I am free."

- On the word "free," extinguish or snuff out the candle and with it the power of the goblins or orcs.

- Hold out the smudge and make a second smoke circle in the reverse direction, but leave a gap at the end of the smoke circle so the energies can disperse.

- Wrap the candle in paper and throw it away in an environmentally friendly way and tip the garlic away under running water.

- Spend time outdoors doing something you enjoy.

- You can repeat the same ritual for the same or different problems. Some people prefer always to work only with one or two goblins. It is better to work slowly and take longer than to push yourself and amplify rather than reduce fears.

## Benign Big Creatures

Some large or ugly creatures are unfairly considered malevolent simply because they are large and ugly, though the tiniest and most ethereal of faeries can on occasion be extremely nasty. Once they are encountered in ritual and meditation, these large beings have protective powers to release us from fear, negativity, bullying, earthly ill-wishing, or seemingly insurmountable challenges.

### Giants

Originally in mythology, giant beings were regarded as creator sky spirits; for example, in Australian aboriginal lore, giants were thought to be the first to walk on the earth.

Legends worldwide would suggest giants were not uncommon in the past. However, in spite of their size, these tall races were no match for the smaller and more mobile iron-weapon-wielding peoples. It may then be that they were banished to the mountains but still assisted the smaller races with heavy work. Because they ate too much and trampled over house and people (albeit inadvertently), they became enemies of humankind and so were enslaved or wiped out. However, their energies remain in high or open places, and are often recalled in local legend or the naming of a rock or cave.

In the oldest myths of Scandinavia, most not recorded until the 1100s CE by the monks, it is told how mighty Thor, the thunder god, waged war against the giants and the trolls with his mighty hammer mjollnir that sounded like thunder. Thor may have been a Viking hero giant, for it is told that he was too heavy to cross the Rainbow Bridge that spanned the dimensions between *Asgard*, the world of the gods, and *Midgard*, the realm of mortals.

With the onset of Christianity, giants became regarded as enemies of the church in many lands, though according to myth they and the larger trolls seem to have been used for the heavy work involved in building churches and cathedrals, and then tricked out of their rightful payment.

## The Chalk Giants of England

In England, giants seem more favoured in folklore. A number of giants in English accounts, especially in Cornwall, were kind and protected their villages from less-friendly giants and other external dangers, for example rescuing local fishing boats from bad storms.

The memory of giant beings is recalled in two huge, white, chalk figures, the Cerne Abbas Giant etched into the hillside of Dorset in the South West of England and the Long Man of Wilmington in East Sussex in the South East. These figures are almost 2,000 years old. They have served in Christian as well as pre-Christian times in folk customs and ceremonies as a source of fertility to humans, animals, and crops.

The Cerne Abbas giant is said to be 180 feet tall with a twenty-seven-foot erect phallus; the Long Man is said to stand at 231 feet tall and 235 feet wide, forming one of the largest humanlike figures in the world.

The Cerne Abbas giant is surrounded by ancient sacred sites. Both Cerne Abbas and the Long Man of Wilmington are created on ley lines. Strange lights and dancing beings have been seen around them, especially during the old fertility festivals of the spring equinox and midsummer that continued right through Christian times.

Wayland's Smithy, a huge dolmen or stone table tomb on the old Ridgeway in Oxfordshire, United Kingdom, is said to be the home of the gigantic Anglo-Saxon blacksmith god who became a folklore giant. This is also on a major ley energy line. Until the late 1800s, Wayland would be left a silver coin so that he would reshod any horse tethered overnight while the owners slept nearby. Many earth nature beings were expert smiths or builders.

## Giants as Slaves

Over time, giantesses in particular seem to have become slaves for humans, for example as in the folk tale of the giantesses who made the sea salt. It is told that Frodi, the king of Denmark, was given a magical mill that would grind anything he wished. So great were the magical grindstones that even his mightiest warriors could not turn them. He therefore bought two giantesses, Menia and Frenia, to be his slaves; they ground gold for him. The land prospered, peace reigned, and the gold overflowed. Yet Frodi would not let the exhausted giantesses rest and in anger they ground an enemy army of Vikings who landed and killed the Danes.

The Viking chief proved an equally cruel master and made the giantesses grind salt on board his ship without rest. Salt was a very valuable cargo that could be exchanged for treasures on their travels. At last Frigg the Goddess took pity on the weary women and avenged the chief's cruelty. The weight of salt was so great it sank the ship and all were drowned. From that time, the sea has been salt and so the gift was shared throughout mankind.

## Absorbing Giant Power

- Visit high mountains, very tall forests, and natural huge boulder formations, sometimes with a giant's name and legend attached. Alternatively, visit the old stone circles whose guardians are gigantic, often shadowy brown beings.

- Look up and picture a being as tall as the tallest tree or as wide as a huge rock or stone and *see* that being radiating light and power. If this is hard, close your eyes and the image will come. Open your eyes and blink, and it will be momentarily before you.

- In a city, look up at a tall cathedral, highrise skyscraper, or a glass observation tower.

- Reach up with your fully extended dominant arm and touch an imaginary finger on the giant. This finger would be longer than your arm.

- Let the light flow into you and say, "I have the power to overcome anything and anybody. I can achieve what I wish to achieve. I can move mountains." Alternatively, push against the trunk of a huge tree or tall, wide rock, especially one named after a giant legend, and again feel the power of the giant within you.

- When you feel powerful and confident, go somewhere open and deserted, preferably high up where you feel on top of the world.

- Open your arms wide, stand tall, and yell your name and newfound power at the top of your voice.

- Thank your giant because you can now achieve almost anything in your daily world. If possible, take a small stone or piece of wood from the giant-power site to carry in your daily life as an amulet to remind you of the giant. Remember to say "until we meet again," because you do not want a huge giant, however benign, trampling your flower patch.

## Ogres

Ogres were made famous by the faery story of "Jack and the Beanstalk" with the ogre's cry, "Fee fi fo fum, I smell the blood of an Englishman" (or an inhabitant of whatever land the story is being recounted). Again, the suggestion is that a mighty being is a cannibal, thereby tapping into our deepest fears.

The ogre is a very large form of orc, an earth being. The name *ogre* comes from the Latin *orcus*, meaning "a god of the underworld." The ogre is a particularly ugly form of giant. He is slightly smaller than an ordinary giant with an eye in the middle of the head and a humped back. One of the sources of this description may be that in less-socially aware times people with physical deformities were treated as outcasts and persecuted, often being driven away into the hills or forests to fend for themselves.

In Norse mythology, ogres create storms by striking their iron clubs against the Earth (and so are not very popular with trolls and other giants) and toss trees and boulders around when angry. However, ogres like trolls can protect wild animals and wildlife against careless or cruel humans.

## Who Is Your Ogre?

We all have an ogre in our lives, whether a tax inspector (apologise to nice ones, of whom there are a lot), your employer, a bully in your life, or a huge problem like crippling debt, a chronic or progressive illness, or loneliness. Fey ogre power can be used to provide strength to overcome these earthly ogres. Ogre magick is especially effective against emotional vampires, people who steal your ideas, or relationships where you feel controlled. It is also brilliant against stalkers or for protection if you live in a dangerous area.

- In the morning, once it is light, go to a rock-strewn place or where there are fallen trees, both of which ogres like to throw. Alternatively find a clearing in a wood.

- Sit down; in your dominant hand, hold a sparkling light fey crystal such as clear quartz or a citrine to protect you from your fears.

- Sit against a rock or fallen tree and explain quietly but firmly aloud or in your mind to your personal ogre that you mean no harm, but that you are not prepared to accept less than fair treatment.

- Name the situation that is worrying you, especially if there does not seem to be a solution to the problems or you feel that there are overwhelming odds against you, whether financially, legally, or a miscarriage of justice. Firmness but politeness is necessary when seeking the help of ogres, as they can try to be petty bullies if they sense you are weak.

• When you are ready, throw your crystal as far as possible straight ahead as you as an offering to the ogre. Say, "Return to me as light and hope. You [name the person, injustice, or problem] are and will be an ogre to me no more. Your power to intimidate me is no more."

• Spend a day of pure pleasure (when did you last do that?).

• When you return to the everyday world, you will find your ogre much easier to deal with.

• Repeat monthly if necessary if you are dealing with a longstanding or complex problem.

## Trolls

Trolls are the most commonly described fearsome beings; there are various historical accounts of sightings through the ages in Scandinavia, Germany, Denmark, Finland, Scotland, Italy, Russia, and Siberia. According to folk tales, their original home was the dark, icy land called Trollebotn. This was the vast, frozen, sea area that joined Greenland to north of Scandinavia at the end of the last Ice Age. They are descendants of the Norse *jotun*, or frost giants.

In modern times, they are rarely sighted except by locals in deep forests or mountainous regions. It has been speculated that as railways, homes, and logging enterprises penetrate deeper into previously unknown tracts of forest, so the troll beings are increasingly remaining underground. They live near lakes, especially remote ones in the middle of forests.

*About Trolls*

Though trolls are of different sizes, most are large, incredibly strong, and quite fearsome in appearance. In Scandinavia, the largest trolls are called *dovregubben*. All are described as having ugly, wrinkled, and fleshy faces, with shaggy hairy and squat bodies and feet. Their hands, feet, and noses are disproportionately large and they have only four fingers and toes on each hand and foot. Some have bushy tails.

Trolls mainly live underground. The entrance to their homes is hidden beneath huge boulders in forests, on lake sides or in the mountains. Some of these boulders are supported, it is said, from beneath by pillars of pure gold. They live in complexes with other trolls and a troll king and queen, and it is there that they avidly count their gold, jewels, and other precious metals. The richer ones live in gold-and-crystal houses. Most cannot stand sunlight and, like dwarves, would be turned into stone if exposed to sunlight. Smaller trolls live in hills or burial mounds.

Some trolls are more homely and marry troll brides and raise families, baking their bread and brewing their beer just like ordinary human families.

The autumn equinox (around September 21 in the Northern Hemisphere and six months earlier for migrant trolls in the Southern Hemisphere) is the major festival of the trolls. On this night they congregate at ancient sites, especially burial mounds.

Apart from sunlight, trolls cannot be easily destroyed, except by lightning (the sparks from Thor's hammer) and they live for hundreds of years. Some smaller trolls can tolerate winter sunlight.

Though they are fierce with a reputation for being bad-tempered, trolls help animals and travelers and are skilful with herbs. They are natural guardians of bridges and highways and as such are very territorial. There are tales of less-friendly trolls or those in a bad mood harassing travelers and demanding tolls or capturing animals who walk over the bridges as in the famous tale of the "Three Billy Goats Gruff".[1]

## Norwegian Mountain Trolls

These are the archetypal trolls, found underground in deep caves near mountain tops along the Norwegian fjords within the sound of the sea. These trolls were immortalised in Henrik Ibsen's play *Peer Gynt*, which was published in 1867, and especially in the music of Edvard Grieg, with such evocative pieces as "In the Hall of the Mountain King" (written as incidental music for Ibsen's play). *Peer Gynt* captured the imagined magnificence of the trolls' underground world.[2] Though troll women are more attractive than their mates, nevertheless the troll princess used her natural shape-shifting ability to convince her would-be bridegroom Peer Gynt she was a lovely maiden (at least until the wedding).

## Icelandic Trolls

Icelandic trolls are unique in that they are often accompanied by very large animals. These huge trolls are seen mainly during the long, dark winters; rock formations have been identified where they have been turned to stone by sunlight. At Hvitserkur on Iceland's northwest coast, a petrified troll's gigantic cow can be seen. The troll abandoned her while she was drinking from the sea and ran for shelter as the sun rose.

## Magical Troll Powers

Among the powers of trolls was the ability to transform themselves into rain and storms, fierce animals, and females into beautiful young women to seduce young men (as in Grieg's "In the Hall of the Mountain King").

Trolls are great fortune-tellers in return for a payment of gold. Like giants, they hurl large stones around, especially at churches. This is not because of a hatred of Christianity but because the church bells remind them of Thor's hammer. Some Scandinavian parishes would in times past ring church bells to keep the trolls away.

# Using the Hammer of Thor to Overcome Troll Energies in Your Life

Thor was himself a giant, the largest of the gods. His hammer, mjollnir, said to have caused lightning when it was thrown, always returned to his hand after hitting its target.

The hammer of Thor is, therefore, a very powerful symbol with which to empower yourself to deal with your particular earthly troll and transform a negative situation to a positive one.

You probably have encountered annoying trolls, people who go out of their way to make life difficult in petty ways, withhold information or services for no good reason, charge us unfairly, or offer shoddy workmanship. They may also be colleagues, friends, or relatives who borrow money and never return it. Or they expect us to babysit at a moment's notice or change our plans at the last minute because they are unhappy or bored.

If you are a nice person you probably, like me, almost never protest at time wasters or whiners who drain you emotionally, much less create flashes of lightning and thunder. But the occasional thunderbolt works wonders against human trolls when there is inefficiency or unhelpfulness.

## The Power of Thor Ritual

- Find two small hand bells, Tibetan bells, or a string of small bells to symbolically drive away the trolls in your life and deter future ones from being attracted to you, often viewing you as a soft touch.

- Ring your bells three times; stomp three times on the ground and name one troll that has been irritating or frustrating you. Say, "[name of troll], I call on you to cease your troublesome behaviour. So does Thor's hammer drive you back underground as sunlight grows. Come no more to trouble me."

- Repeat the words and actions until you have named as many trolls as come to mind, past ones as well as present that may be keeping you awake and fuming, or disturbing your peace of mind by loading you with guilt.

- Finally, ring the bells three more times, stamp on the ground three more times and say, "By the thud of Thor's mighty hammer do I protect my life from your irritations. Remain underground, you trolls, until you can be helpful. When you can return in welcome, in the name of Thor and his victorious hammer."

- Next time there is a storm, watch the thunder and lightning and recall the power of Thor.

- If you wish, draw a Thurisaz (Thor's rune) on the palm of your dominant hand, using the index finger of the other hand and in front of the computer or iPad screen before answering a confrontational email. Thurisaz represents the mighty Hammer of the giant Thor. If a caller on the phone proves to be troublesome, etch the rune in the air with your free hand in front of the receiver or mobile to send back negativity and have the confidence to stand your ground.

## Can We Create Nature Beings?

The answer is probably yes. Should we? The answer is definitely not, unless you create a positive protective thought as suggested below for a limited time, within definite parameters, and always for good. This section, the last in the book, is in many ways the most important, for it brings the awareness that nature beings are separate from us and because of their unpredictability and ambivalence are not to be manipulated or used.

There are some terrifying historical accounts of people who throughout history have animated clay or mud using the undiluted elemental powers of nature and the golem is perhaps the most fearsome form. I certainly would tell anyone to avoid making one of these, as not only do you need advanced knowledge of Hebrew mysticism, but in the unlikely event you succeeded because a malevolent nature spirit harnessed the pure elemental power, you could end up very psychologically damaged and haunted if your golem decided not to play ball and return to the clay.

## The Golem

The creation of a golem by Rabbi Abba ben Rav Hamma is first recorded in the Babylonian Talmud around the fourth century CE, though it is known the brothers of Joseph and Abraham made them as well as animal and humanoid golems. Abraham is said to have lived 1812 to 1637 BCE.

The golem is not a ghost. He is a pure, elemental earth spirit given a form by a human (golems are male), and is able to acquire superhuman strength. A statue of the most famous golem can be seen at the entrance to the former Jewish Quarter in Prague. It is told that in 1580 CE, according to legend, Judah Loew ben Bezalel, a wise and very learned rabbi in the ghetto of Prague, created a golem to protect his persecuted people. He formed the golem from shapeless clay with the intention it would live as long as the Jewish people were threatened by prejudice and violence, purely as a defender. When the people were safe, the golem would return to lifeless clay. As the golem fought to defend the Jews, the golem grew so huge that the Hebrew word *emet* ("truth"), written in Hebrew letters to animate him, engraved upon his forehead, could no longer be seen. In time, the golem became a danger to everyone.

For even the most skilful practitioner has problems because the pure elemental is by nature untameable, and creating a humanlike body to be animated by the elemental nature force will mean the body just grows and becomes out of control. In a sense, the golem achieved his purpose as the emperor promised to protect the Jews in return for the golem's destruction.

The wise Rabbi Judah Loew ben Bezalel had a huge struggle to finally deactivate the Prague golem by wiping with a single stroke the forehead word *emet* to *met*, which means "death." This is the danger of giving form to elemental spirits who are pure, uncontained energy and do not have a permanent habitat and a lifestyle to dilute the energies.[3]

# Creating a Magical Earth
# Elemental Being for Healing

The tradition of creating elemental nature beings exists outside formal mono-
theistic religions. In ancient Egypt from the 3000 BCE, clay or Nile mud was
shaped into crocodiles or scorpions and animated by magical words to protect
against enemies or achieve revenge.

True elemental spirits only take a nature-spirit form for a particular purpose and specific time which can vary from a few minutes to a thousand years.
Think of the wildest ocean, the fiercest tempest, the bush fire, or an earthquake—part of Mother Earth's constant pattern of creation, destruction and
renewal. That is elemental power, and so working with earth is the most stable
and safest.

If used only for healing and returned to its element and shapelessness
immediately after the ritual, any earth elemental, be it crocodile or golem
figure, can be used to transmit healing from Mother Earth, especially in cases
of pain, obsession, or when conventional means have failed. Work always and
only for the highest purpose and the purest intention.

## Making Clay Images to Tap the Power
## of Mother Earth and the Earth Elementals

By actually forming an elemental nature being figure from clay or dough and
etching words of power on the clay or dough and reciting them, you can,
without offending the laws of morality, focus your own intentions and help
to lessen an addiction or destructive emotional bond. In this way, you can
psychically as well as psychologically banish fear and awaken determination
to be free. You can do this for others as well as yourself.

Where some practitioners believe you should ask permission before healing, I believe it is acceptable to send healing as long as you ask the person's
angels and guides to use the healing you send as is best, especially if the person
is vulnerable, young, with a clouded mind, or encased in an obsession. This

may mean that the person unconsciously chooses to keep illness or pain for a time as part of their karmic path. All we are doing is sending healing as an offering with the highest intention.

- The clay forms the conduit for the elemental earth strength.

- First, decide on the image you wish to create of the earth elemental being, depending on the nature of the illness or obsession. It should be small, no taller than the distance between your wrist to index fingertip, and without features. If you choose, you can give the being wings (for example, if the person is claustrophobic) or a mermaid tail (if there is a drinking issue). You can add fire by studding the body with tiny yellow glass nuggets or citrine crystal chips (to fill with light if, for example, there is a deep depression).

- Use either the kind of clay you buy in a craft store, children's play clay or dough, or you can make a basic dough with plain flour, water and a little cooking oil such as sunflower to make it pliant.

- As you are working with the dough, make sure you work in sunlight (or at least daylight) and move your fingers rhythmically saying, "Light enter this dough that I may create beauty, healing, and goodness and work only for higher purposes without malice or malevolence. I welcome you wise elementals for a short time and with blessings to aid my endeavour."

- Whisper this over and over in a steady rhythm. You need make only small quantities and store the rest if you want to repeat the healing daily for an acute or complex matter. Avoid knives and use wooden implements where possible. Work outdoors if possible.

- If the problem is a fatal attraction between two people or an abusive relationship, make two figures and set them back to back.

## Empowering the Image

- Once you have created the image or images, empower them with the purpose of the ritual. Light a red candle directly behind the image.

- Sprinkle a few drops of salt water over the image, then a few drops more of rose or lavender essential oil or perfume, the light a floral incense stick in cedar or myrrh and pass it around the image in a square for protection (twice clockwise and twice counterclockwise), for each saying, "I purify this clay and my heart from all negative intent. May only good reside within."

- Now make a circle of incense smoke around you to enclose also the table you are working on, three times in each direction, starting three times counterclockwise if you live in the Southern Hemisphere and clockwise for the Northern Hemisphere.

- Finally, take your incense censer or stick and facing south this time pass it in a cross from south to north and then east to west, then southeast to northwest and southwest to northeast, to form a star shape in smoke, saying, "Wise being formed from earth, bring the healing so earnestly desired [name precisely the purpose needed] and carry your restorative powers to [name or myself] if right and good it is to be."

- Hold the image over the candle and say, "Light the way to healing."

- Blow three times softly in the flame with the image still over the candle, repeating, "Light the way to healing."

- Spiral the incense in all directions over the image, repeating softly as often as feels right, "Light the way to healing."

- Now clap three times and blow out the candle to animate the image with fire, saying for the final time, "Light the way to healing."

- Now roll the clay or dough back into a ball, after removing any nuggets or crystals, saying, "May all be as it was before. Wise elementals return to your own element with blessings and thanks until we meet again."

- Leave the incense to burn; if not outdoors, go outdoors and bury the clay where nothing is growing, just bare soil.

- You can repeat the ritual up to five times in a week for as long as necessary.

---

Chapter 9 Sources

1. Galdone, Paul. *The Three Billy Goats Gruff*. New York: Sandpiper, 1981.

2. Peer Gynt, http://ebooks.adelaide.edu.au/i/ibsen/henrik/peer/

3. http://www.prague.net/golem

# appendix

～～

# THE TREASURY
# OF FAERY WISDOM

This section is a collection of useful information about faeries and nature spirits that will help you to understand the structure of fey magick and to create your own rituals. I have collected this over many years from a variety of sources, especially oral myths and local stories as I have traveled the world.

## Animals and Faeries

Faeries and nature beings are kindred spirits of animals, especially wild ones, and may act as their protectors. For example, the Norwegian wood nymph, *skogsfru*, portrayed as a beautiful woman living deep in the forest, traditionally acts as caretaker of the woods and wild woodland animals; for example, she protects young moose when they are abandoned by their mother.

Many nature spirits shape shift or take the form of different animals. The German kobold, a small, black dwarf figure either acts as household protector or lives underground and assists miners; the kobold has been reported in the form of wet cats, hens, bats, roosters, snakes, worms, or martens (chapter 3).

## Changelings

Faeries were frequently blamed for exchanging a beautiful mortal child for a hideously ugly and often disabled child who could not speak or move properly. The mortal child could only be restored, it was believed, either by tricking the faery changeling to speak or more brutally by beating or burning it so that the faery mother would be unable to watch and restore the real infant, saying, "Harm not my child for I never harmed yours."

There are few records of how many apparently disabled mortal children assumed to be faery changelings were killed by superstitious parents in days when disability was far more common, with poor standards of nutrition and the hazards of childbirth. As late as 1843 the *West Briton* newspaper in Cornwall, UK, reported the case of a John Trevelyan of Penzance who was charged with ill-treating one of his children. The child, who was not quite three, was, according to witnesses, regularly kicked and beaten by the parents and the servants and from fifteen months old had been left to live outside for hours at a time, even in the coldest winter and at Christmas. The parents' defence was that he was not their child but a changeling and the case against them was dismissed on a technicality. The magistrates agreed the child had been cruelly treated and the family was forced to leave town because of hostility. Yet John Trevelyan was not a poor ignorant man, for his name was given the title of esquire after it, indicating he had some local standing and he had at least two servants.

The German Protestant reformer Martin Luther (1483 to 1546) encouraged such beliefs by declaring that Satan was responsible for the exchange of healthy infants for malformed fey ones and that such changelings were children of the devil, were just pieces of flesh and did not have souls. Occasionally a child or young adult was brutally treated or even killed during an exorcism in an attempt to remove the devil from them.

# Crystals and Faeries

Faeries love all crystals, especially sparkling ones. Most popular are amethyst, chiastolite, chlorite phantoms, citrine, clear quartz, epidote, flint, garnet, any of the fluorites, holey stones, lodalite, moonstones, opals (precious, Andean, or the Australian boulder opal), pearls, rose quartz, selenite, siderite, and staurolite. The ones listed below have especially powerful fey associations and so can be used in faery rituals and as offerings.

## Chiastolite

Usually grey with black or brown equal-armed cross inclusion; can also form yellow-brown cross in other minerals.

Chiastolite comes from China. It has become associated with the powers of the four winds and so can be used to attract air nature spirits. It is considered a bridge between dimensions and so is very protective and can be worn or carried not only to see the fey people of any culture, but also to act as protection against malevolent ones. It is believed to bring good fortune if carried in a purse as a charm.

## Chlorite Phantom Crystal

Quartz crystal with a chlorite phantom or faint crystal outline or occasionally clear quartz phantom enclosed by chlorite, both caused when the inner crystal stopped growing. Usually pale green, watery, or clear white with pale green inner ghost; the greenness depends on the amount of chlorite. This phantom reveals nature creatures that live under the earth. Go to a forested hillside or cave opening as the light is fading; sit with your phantom chlorite to connect with tree and earth energies that are sensed or seen by children and some adults; such as dwarves, tree spirits, gnomes, and elves. Said to be the perfect balance of sky and earth, in myths of many cultures, chlorite phantom quartz has formed a home for faeries or earth spirits. Much treasured as protective house guardians, it is kept near the hearth. Set herbs, essential oils, homeopathic remedies, or plant essences you intend to use for healing close to your chlorite phantom for a few hours to enhance the natural energies with the power of the fey.

## Epidote
Usually olive green, pale to dark green, yellowish or brownish green, and brown to black. To attract the abundance of the faeries, create a fey health and abundance layout in your home, either in your indoor or outdoor place with a piece of natural epidote in the centre and an equal-armed cross of green crystals including epidote tumblestones in each of the arms.

## Flint
Usually black, brown, or grey but can be a variety of other colours depending upon impurities. Flint arrowheads gained the name "elf shot" after mediaeval country dwellers found these prehistoric flint tools and arrowheads in ploughed fields and believed faeries had dropped them. If you do find a flint tool or arrow it is incredibly lucky; it is said that the finder of a flint tool is granted a single fey wish. Three flint arrowheads, pointing outward to create a triangle around a dish of coins found in pockets or bags draws small but regular amounts of money to the home; use the coins regularly, but make sure the dish is never empty.

## Naturally Holey or Holed Stones
Any stone with a natural hole caused by water or weathering, usually in limestone; brown, fawn, grey, or white is well worth finding, usually on a river bank or seashore. Traditionally, it was believed that looking through the hole of a natural stone at midnight on full moon gives sight of faeries, nature spirits, and ghosts. Also called "Odin stones" in Scandinavia and "hag stones" or "witch stones" the north of England, naturally holed stones have a long magical history in many different cultures. Holed stones protect against paranormal harm, ill-wishes, and those who seek to control our minds; traditionally kept near the front door to guard the home, again on a red knotted cord or on the bedpost to repel nightmares, malevolent nature spirits and psychic attack

while asleep. A long, pointed, holed stone was probably the earliest pendulum. If you can find one, use it on red cord as a pendulum for following faery paths.

## Lodalite or Dream Crystal

Clear with mixed-colour mineral inclusions; often brownish inside like tendrils with a clear dome of quartz enclosing them. Look within a lodalite dome and see forests, faeries, elves, fey palaces, and forest revels. Especially good for sitting outdoors and seeing fey worlds under the earth. Lodalite also has associations with gardens. Keep one in the centre of your garden to attract birds, wildlife, gnomes, dwarves, and tree and plant spirits.

## Siderite

Usually brown, tan, pale yellow, brownish yellow, greenish brown, reddish brown, and sometimes iridescent or pearly. A crystal carried traditionally to protect against bad faeries, elves, and mischievous nature spirits, siderite is an amulet against bad luck, the carelessness of others, breakages, breakdown of vehicles or equipment, and accidents.

## Staurolite, also Known as "Faery Tears" or "Faery Cross"

Usually reddish brown, dark brown, black, or yellowish brown and streaked with white; gradually weathers to grey. The cross formation represents the four elements of earth, air, fire, and water that in magick are believed to combine to create the fifth element called Aether or Akasha. Touch the four points of the cross whenever you need fey energies in your life. Staurolite has been prized since ancient times as a lucky charm and a protective talisman for travelers, including the crusaders and the former president Franklin Delano Roosevelt. In myth, faery crosses were the frozen tears of faeries or earth angels who wept at the crucifixion of Jesus. Take staurolite outdoors to connect with nature essences even in the centre of a city. Staurolite provides a gentle and protective shield against negativity, helping to raise our spirits and lift us out of depression.

# Faery Flowers

All flowers with bells are faery flowers as are all small petal flowers wherever they grow, whether in green lands or in the desert after rain. Generally, fey flowers are pastel colours, though the colours will be stronger in areas of strong earth energies, such as rainforests. Fragranced flowers are especially attractive to faeries, from the exotic frangipani and hibiscus to more temperate lavender and roses. Both wild and cultivated flowers attract faeries.

## Bluebells

Fields of bluebells are associated with faery enchantment. The bells ring to call faeries to their revels at midnight and on the faery festivals. For this reason, bluebells should not be picked. Because faeries hang spells on bluebells, you should avoid walking through a field or woodland of bluebells because if you trample on them it is said the faeries will be angry and spirit you away.

## Cowslips, also Called "Faery Cups"

With small yellow flowers on each stamen, cowslips grow in clusters and faeries sleep in the drooping bells. They reveal faery gold buried nearby, but the gold should not be disturbed; any gold found will disappear at dawn. In Christian times, they are linked with St. Peter and said to symbolize his keys to the kingdom of heaven.

## Daisies

Daisy chains were traditionally draped around children's necks to protect them from being stolen by the faeries. According to Roman myth, the daisy was created by the forest nymph Belides when she transformed herself into a daisy to escape from the amorous Vertumnus, god of the orchards.

## Dandelions

Said to be a form taken on by sun faeries to prevent careless humans treading on them. Faeries travel on dandelion spores and if you send faeries on their way by blowing a dandelion clock, then you may have one wish. The same is true of thistles.

## Ferns
Linked to elves and pixies which hide in ferns to eavesdrop on mortals; as such, the little people should be spoken of respectfully when near to them.

## Foxgloves
The purple or white cups of foxgloves are worn as hats by faeries. "Fox" is a corruption of "folk," as in "the cups of the good folk." Foxgloves are called "faery gloves" in Wales and "faery bells" in Ireland. The whole flower acts as shelter for tiny faeries and so foxgloves should not be transplanted since it may well be home for a faerie. Handle carefully because they are poisonous if eaten.

## Lilies-of-the-Valley
According to Irish myth, Lilies-of-the-Valley act as ladders for faeries to climb in order to reach the reeds from which they plait their cradles. When Lilies-of-the-Valley are found in forests, you will often notice a number of doorways in the trees and creepers linking different levels between the trees. You should not pick Lilies-of-the-Valley in forests.

## Lilies
Each lily contains its own flower faery that survives only the life of the flower and so should not be picked (keep them in soil as plants). The water lily is said to grow where water faeries play and that particularly beautiful nymphs take the form of water lilies to avoid the attentions of unwanted suitors.

## Primroses
Primroses are yellow, white, pink, and purple, though most commonly yellow. They are sacred both to the mother Goddess and the Celtic druids. Place five freshly gathered primroses found near water, which opens the way to faery-land, especially when placed on an ancient sacred stone. Primroses growing

around a tree can conceal a door to faeryland. Place a bunch on the doorstep to bring the blessings of the faery folk into the home.

## Thyme

A magical herb, said to increase the vision of faeries if eaten. Plant near doors and windows to invite the faery folk to bring you prosperity. Sprinkle the dried herb around windows and the doorstep to attract benign home guardians; said to grow naturally where earth energies are strongest and so a natural place to see faeries.

## Vervain

This is an old north country English custom, but is found in similar form in other places around the globe. The wizard's herb, said to be protective to drive away malevolent nature spirits and evil witches. A wreath of yellow St. John's Wort, trefoil, vervain, and dill was plaited and hung on doors at midsummer with the words written: *Trefoil, vervain, St. John's Wort, dill, drive off bad spirits at your will.*

The wreath keeps its power until it disintegrates. Vervain grown in pots or the garden attracts the blessings of nature spirits and guardians of the land on which even urban homes and offices are built.

# Mutual Dependency of Faeries on Humans

Faeries often sought the help of women when they were giving birth. Sanna, a woman I met recently in the UK who has a Finnish family, told me that in her local folk custom, small, oddly shaped fey creatures called *kirkonwaki* (a word that means "church folk" in Finnish) live underneath church altars. An intuitive woman who senses that a female kirkonwaki is experiencing a difficult labor will place her hand on the altar to take away the faerie's pain. Traditionally, the mortal woman is rewarded with money, good luck, or unexpected good news very soon afterward.

In April 1660, a Swedish clergyman living near Ragunda named Reverend Rahm told of a troll-like man who came to the door and asked the clergyman's wife to come and help deliver his wife's baby. Reverend Rahm described the figure as small, dark-complexioned, dressed in grey, and distinctly not human. He realised the man was a vetter or nature spirit of the kind that frequented the area. His wife described how she seemed to be carried along by the wind and ended in a dark chamber where she delivered a tiny troll-like baby and then found herself carried home on the wind. Though the incident seemed to take only seconds she was in fact away for hours. The next morning, there was silver left on the mantle shelf of their parsonage.

## Offerings to Faeries

Until the nineteenth century, it was common for offerings to be left for faeries in fields and near homes so the crops would grow and the larders be full. However, those who believe in the fey will still leave gifts and may be rewarded by glimpses of the fey and good luck will increase.

Josiane was on Magnetic Island off the Townsville Coast in Queensland, Australia. One morning, she and her adult son, Daniel, came across a faery ring of inedible mushrooms that had sprung up overnight. They left offerings—flowers and small fruits—and were rewarded with seeing blue faeries she described as having blue petal-fringed faces, dancing within the circle.

### Times to See Faeries, According to Different Traditions

- Each twenty-four-hour period has its transition times, when the sun is at its height or night prevails, sunrise, noon, sunset (or some say the hour before), the beginning of the Celtic day, and midnight. These are very potent times to see the fey.

- Fridays are associated with faeries. Friday is the day of Frigga, the Norse mother Goddess and protector of faeries, when more traditional fey beings hold sway. For this reason, you should not cut your hair or nails on a Friday or it is said the faeries will use the clippings to play tricks on you.

- Thursday is the sabbath of the trolls and all larger or wilder nature spirits as well as household guardians, especially in Scandinavia.

- The full moon is a highly magical time. Another magical time is when the moon is passing through Scorpio each month, an event that can last for up to two and a half days. When the moon in Cancer and Pisces, both water signs like Scorpio, are other fey times and also for ghost sightings. As I have discovered from the informal studies I have carried out, these findings are especially intense on lines or spots of earth energy.

## Trees and Faeries

### Alder

The alder tree, like the willow, grows by water and is associated both with tree spirits and the water fey. There is said to be an entrance to the lands of the fey. Alder faeries may fly as ravens and are very protective of nature.

### Ash

Ash nymphs were, in ancient Greece, regarded as cloud goddesses. Wherever an ash tree grows it is considered to offer access to faeryland, especially if gnarled.

Ash-tree spirits are common wherever there are ash trees; ash berries were supposed to be protective against an infant being taken as a changeling.

The luck of the ash faeries could be transferred for seven days by carrying a small ash twig with an even number of leaves on each side, plucked with the spoken words, "Even ash I do thee pluck, seeking thus to have good luck," and then stating the purpose. Afterward, this twig must be returned to the place from where it was plucked. Ash can be used in faery healing rituals.

# Elder

The elder is the ultimate faery tree. It is said that if you wear a crown of elder twigs on May Eve (April 30 in the Northern Hemisphere and October 31 in the Southern Hemisphere), you will be able to see these magical creatures. Native Americans call the elder the "tree of music." So potent is the elder whistle that nature spirits are said to dance to its tune. In Wales, a cap woven from hazel twigs allows the wearer to see faeries, and if you see them they will grant wishes.

## Dried Elderberries as Part of an Incense Mix to Attract Faeries

The female spirit who inhabits the elder tree, especially in Western Europe and Scandinavia, is associated with wise women because of its gentle healing properties. The tree spirit is called *holun tar* (tree of the crone goddess Holla) in Germany, *hyllemoer* ("elder mother" in Danish), and the similar *hyldermoder* in Sweden. Holla, hulda or Mother Holle is said to care for unborn children in her cave as well as those who died young. She is said to pick the first berries of the summer for them. In later traditions, she was regarded as a wise faery godmother.

# Hawthorn

Another major faery tree sometimes called "the witches' tree," you may see faeries if you sit beneath one during the twilight hours. But do not shelter under one on the faery festivals May, Midsummer Eve, or Halloween, because you will become enchanted by the faeries. Single thorns growing near faery hills and those in threes are especially magical. Hawthorn should never be cut except when in bloom and traditionally hawthorn or May blossoms may only be taken indoors on May mornings when they bring fertility and prosperity to the home. A hawthorn will protect a home against lightning if planted in the garden.

# Oak

Oaks are said to attract whole colonies of faeries to live within and acorns which provide both food and adornments for celebrations, especially autumn ones. Acorn shells are used as faery cups and hats. Try the following fey spell for love. You will need an acorn with a cup attached (always use fallen acorns that have been discarded by the faeries to avoid being accused of stealing) and a sprig of ash leaves with seeds (or keys). Wrap the ash leaves around the acorn and bury both, if possible between an oak and ash tree, otherwise where a clump of trees is growing. As you work, say six times, "Dying leaves may blow away, but my love is here to stay. Acorn cup and ashen key, may we long together married be." You can also use this to call an as-yet unknown love or one who has gone away.

## Rowan or Mountain Ash

The rowan or mountain ash was regarded as protective against enchantment by wicked witches and nasty fey folk.

Rowan crosses that were not cut with iron (for fear of upsetting good faeries) were tied with red twine and placed on barns and outhouses every May morning to keep bad faeries away for the upcoming year. A rowan twig was tied to a cow's tail to stop faeries from stealing the milk. Using a rowan churn would also prevent the butter from going rancid. Rowan cradles were said to protect babies from being stolen by the faeries, as did a wreath of mistletoe.

## Willow

Willow trees are associated with both moon and water faeries that may be seen dancing in full moonlight. Traditionally, willow faeries will leave their trees and follow travelers to guide them, but if they are feeling mischievous, they will create the illusion of the actual tree moving. A circle of willows makes the most magical faery circle of all, and one you can stand within and carry out fey rituals.

# Ways to Keep Less Benign
# Nature Beings Out of Homes

## Iron

Iron and steel are metals feared by all nature spirits. In many lands, women who had just given birth would have nails hammered at the base board of the bed in order to protect mothers from being kidnapped to act as wet nurses for faery babies or their newborn infants from being stolen and exchanged for sickly faery babies.

It may not be helpful to attack faeries with sharp iron, not only because it angers them but also many nature spirits are vulnerable beings, even large, ugly ones. We should learn to be considerate to all creatures which share the planet, even if we need to be wary about some of them.

## Fire

Fire is naturally repellent to faeries (except of course for the fire spirits). For this reason, bonfires are lit on Halloween, when it was believed the dimensions were opened and faeries and nature spirits waited to trick unwary humans. Jack o' lanterns, originally made from turnips and swedes in the old world, and later from pumpkins in America and Australia, were lit to drive away malevolence.

# SUGGESTED READING

Backster, Clive. *Primary Perception: Biocommunication with Plants, Living Foods and Human Cells.* Anza, CA: White Rose Millennium Press, 2003.

Bourke, Angela. *The Burning of Bridget Cleary.* New York: Viking Press, 2000.

Christiansen, Reidar Thoralf, ed. *Folktales of Norway.* Chicago: University of Chicago Press, 1968.

Eason, Cassandra. *A Complete Guide to Fairies and Magical Beings.* New York: Piatkus, 2001.

Evans-Wentz, W. Y. *The Fairy Faith in Celtic Countries.* New York: Lemma Books, 1973.

Forest, Danu. *Nature Spirits, Wyrd Lore, and Wild Fey Magick.* Glastonbury, UK: Wooden Books, 2008.

Franklin, Anna. *The Illustrated Encyclopaedia of Fairies.* Londong: Paper Tiger, 2004.

Froud, Brian, and Jessica Macbeth. *The Faeries' Oracle.* New York: Fireside, 2000.

Geddes, Ward Alice. *Faery Lore.* Composed and performed by Llewellyn. Llewellyn Music US, 2006.

Harvey, Ralph. *Simply Fairies*. New York: Sterling, 2008.

Hephaestus Books. *Atmospheric Ghost Lights, Including: Will-O'-The-Wisp, Marfa Lights, Naga Fireballs, Hessdalen Light, Min Min Light, Brown Mountain Lights, Fireship of Baie Des Chaleurs, the Spooklight, Light of Saratoga, Maco Light, Earthquake Light, Paulding Light*. Hephaestus Books, 2011.

Kirk, Robert, and Andrew Lang. *The Secret Commonwealth of Elves, Fauns and Fairies*. New York: Dover, 2008.

Mack, Carol K., and D. Mack. *A Field Guide to Demons, Vampires, Fallen Angels and Other Subversive Spirits*. New York: Arcade Publishing, 2011.

Matthews, John and Caitlin. *The Encyclopaedia of Magical Creatures: The Ultimate A to Z of Fantastic Beings from Myth and Magic*. New York: Sterling, 2005.

O'Becker, Robert, and Gary Selden. *The Body Electric: Electromagnetism and the Foundation of Life*. New York: HarperCollins, 1998.

Ostrander, Sheila, and Lynne Schroeder. *Psychic Discoveries behind the Iron Curtain*. Englewood Cliffs, NJ: Prentice Hall, 1970.

Pogacnik, Marko. *Nature Spirits and Elemental Beings: Working with the Intelligence in Nature*. Scotland, UK: Findhorn Press, 2009.

Rose, Carol. *Spirits, Fairies, Leprechauns, and Goblins: An Encyclopedia*. New York: Norton, 1998.

Sullivan, Danny. *Ley Lines: the Greatest Landscape Mystery*. Somerset, UK: Green Magic, 2005.

Tolkien, J. R. R. *The Hobbit, or There and Back Again*. New York: Mariner Books, 1999.

———. *The Lord of the Rings*. New York: Houghton-Miffin, 2004.

Tompkins, Peter, and Christopher Bird. *The Secret Life of Plants.* New York: HarperCollins, 1989.

Varner, Gary R. *Sacred Wells: A Study in the History, Meaning and Mythology of Holy Wells and Waters.* Washington, DC: Publish America, 2002.

# INDEX

**A**

Abatwa, 149, 150

Aine, 88

Apheliotes, 122, 124, 126, 127

Arthur, King, 82, 196, 197

**B**

Banshee, 47, 69, 70, 80

Blue Caps, 146

Bokwus, 6, 200

Boreas, 122, 124–27

Borrowing, 23, 64

Brownies, 2, 60–62, 76

Bunyip, 4, 200, 201

Burial Mound, 15, 16, 66

Butterfly Goddess, 109, 114

Bendith Y Mamau, 28, 198

**C**

Chalk Giants, 212

Clionda, 48

Coblynau, 147

Curupira, 206

**D**

Dama Dagenda, 206

Daoine Sidh, 82

Devil, 40, 42, 147, 205, 207, 208, 228

Djinn, 89, 156, 162

Dragons, 155, 157, 165–67, 207

Dwarves, 20, 141, 142, 144, 145, 150, 207, 217, 229, 231

**E**

Earth Lights, 156, 172, 175, 176

Elf Shot, 116, 230

Elementals, 222, 223, 225

El Tio, 6, 147, 148

Elves, 5, 27, 57–66, 73, 74, 80,
    85, 115–18, 150, 151, 207,
    229, 231, 233

    *Dark Elves, 150*

    *Light Elves, 5, 115, 116, 118*

Erl, 150, 153

Elf King, 116, 150

**F**

Faery

    *Crystals, 19, 28*

    *Courts, 81, 82*

    *Doors, 131*

    *Flowers, 232*

    *Gifts, 25, 83*

    *Godmother, 7, 81, 99–102, 237*

    *Journal, 25*

    *Music, 83, 84*

    *Rings, 46*

    *Trees 236–38*

Finvarra, 83, 86, 89

Folletti, 105, 113, 114, 119, 128

Folletto, 113

Fossegrim, 193, 194

Freyr, 115

**G**

Galadriel, 86, 94, 115, 132

Gandalf, 115

Gans, 46

Gaob, 122

Geb, 86, 132

Genie, 163, 164

Giantesses, 213

Giants, 145, 211–13, 215, 218

Goblins, 28, 153, 205, 207–11

Golem, 220–22, 225

Gnomes, 4, 20, 59, 132,
    141–43, 145, 229, 231

Grainne, 88

Greenteeth, Jenny, 203

Gwragedd Annwyn, 197

**H**

Hulda, 237

Huldre, 61, 117

**I**

Icelandic Trolls, 218

Iron, 8, 18, 19, 102, 148, 151,
    152, 157, 197, 215, 238, 239

## J

Jinn, 162, 163

## K

Kiliakai, 206

Knockers, 146, 147

Korreds, 134

Korrigans, 4

Korrs, 134, 151

## L

Lady of the Lake, 196, 197, 199

Leprechaun, 75, 98, 99

Ley Lines, 14, 16, 41, 135, 172, 212

## M

Mab, 87

Maeve, 87

Makalipon, 137

Manannan mac Lir, 90, 91

Mermaids, 6, 180, 184–87

Merpeople, 184, 185, 190

Mimi, 44, 150

Mine Spirits, 146, 148

Moss Wives, 138, 139

## N

Naiads, 192, 193, 202

Naree Pon, 137

Nereides, 183, 184, 202

Nibelungen, 145, 146

Nixes, 199

Nokken, 199

Norwegian Mountain Trolls, 218

Notus, 122, 124, 126, 127

Nunnehi, 46, 136

## O

Oberon, 82, 87, 89

Ogres, 214–16

Oonagh, 9, 83, 86

Orcs, 1, 207–11

Oreads, 193

## P

Paralda, 87, 95, 106

Pixies, 151, 233

Puck, 82, 88, 89, 94

## R

Ran, 4, 40, 44, 79, 91, 218

**S**

Salamander, 156, 160, 161, 176

Selkies, 185, 187, 190

Shakespeare, William, 82

Sielulintu, 105

Simbi, 4, 44, 45, 55

Skogsfru, 227

Sylphs, 6, 34, 106, 109–14, 119, 128

**T**

Titania, 82, 87, 89

Tolkien, 5, 86, 115, 132, 207

Tree Mothers, 139

Trolls, 4, 212, 215–20, 236

Tuatha de Dannan, 82

Tylwyth Teg, 28, 198

**U**

Undines, 179, 182–184

**W**

Will o' the Wisp, 177

**Y**

Yûñwï Tsunsdi, 136, 137, 153

**Z**

Zephyrus, 123, 124, 126, 127

# GET MORE AT LLEWELLYN.COM

Visit us online to browse hundreds of our books and decks, plus sign up to receive our e-newsletters and exclusive online offers.

- Free tarot readings • Spell-a-Day • Moon phases
- Recipes, spells, and tips • Blogs • Encyclopedia
- Author interviews, articles, and upcoming events

# GET SOCIAL WITH LLEWELLYN

**Find us on Facebook**
www.Facebook.com/LlewellynBooks

**Follow us on twitter™**
www.Twitter.com/Llewellynbooks

# GET BOOKS AT LLEWELLYN

## LLEWELLYN ORDERING INFORMATION

**Order online:** Visit our website at www.llewellyn.com to select your books and place an order on our secure server.

**Order by phone:**
- Call toll free within the U.S. at 1-877-NEW-WRLD (1-877-639-9753)
- Call toll free within Canada at 1-866-NEW-WRLD (1-866-639-9753)
- We accept VISA, MasterCard, and American Express

**Order by mail:**
Send the full price of your order (MN residents add 6.875% sales tax) in U.S. funds, plus postage and handling to: Llewellyn Worldwide, 2143 Wooddale Drive Woodbury, MN 55125-2989

**POSTAGE AND HANDLING:**
STANDARD: (U.S. & Canada)
(Please allow 12 business days)
$25.00 and under, add $4.00.
$25.01 and over, FREE SHIPPING.

INTERNATIONAL ORDERS (airmail only):
$16.00 for one book, plus $3.00 for each additional book.

Visit us online for more shipping options. Prices subject to change.

## FREE CATALOG!

To order, call
1-877-NEW-WRLD
ext. 8236
or visit our website

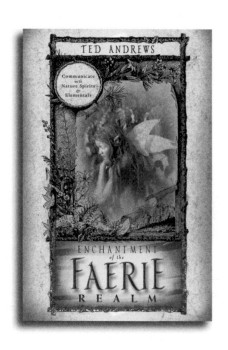

TED ANDREWS

Communicate
with
Nature Spirits
&
Elementals

ENCHANTMENT
of the
FAERIE
REALM

## Enchantment of the Faerie Realm
### *Communicate with Nature Spirits & Elementals*
#### TED ANDREWS

Nothing fires the imagination more than the idea of faeries and elves. *Enchantment of the Faerie Realm* offers practical, in-depth methods for recognizing, contacting, and working with the faerie world. Through patience, persistence and Ted Andrew's instructions, readers can learn to recognize the presence of faeries, nature spirits, devas, elves, and elementals. Also included are personal accounts of the author's experiences with the faerie world.

978-0-87542-002-8, 240 pp., 6 x 9                     $14.95

**To order, call 1-877-NEW-WRLD**
Prices subject to change without notice
Order at Llewellyn.com 24 hours a day, 7 days a week!

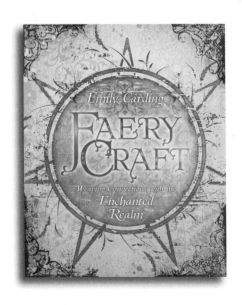

Emily Carding

FAERY CRAFT

Weaving Connections with the
Enchanted
Realm

# Faery Craft
## *Weaving Connections with the Enchanted Realm*
### Emily Carding

*Faery Craft* offers a glittering introduction to the Fae and the people who love them. You'll find nearly 200 beautiful photographs and illustrations, and simple yet effective ideas on how to engage with this wondrous realm. This gorgeous guidebook explores all things Faery, from the amazing variety of magical beings to natural gateways to the Faery realm. Discover how to practice Faery spirituality and magic, create altars, and find a Faery ally. Brimming over with practical advice, *Faery Craft* features an original Faery zodiac, guidance on Faery etiquette and prohibitions, and instructions on how to find your own unique gifts and place in the Faery world.

Those already enchanted by Faery beings will love the book's original art, meditations, and poetry, as well as interviews with Faery authors, artists, and musicians, including R. J. Stewart, John and Caitlín Matthews, Brian and Wendy Froud, Linda Ravenscroft, S. J. Tucker, and Charles de Lint.

**978-0-7387-3133-9, 360 pp., 7½ x 9⅛**                    **$18.99**

**To order, call 1-877-NEW-WRLD**
Prices subject to change without notice
**Order at Llewellyn.com 24 hours a day, 7 days a week!**